On the Way to Diplomacy

BORDERLINES

A BOOK SERIES CONCERNED WITH REVISIONING GLOBAL POLITICS
Edited by David Campbell and Michael J. Shapiro

Volume 7 Costas M. Constantinou, *On the Way to Diplomacy*

Volume 6 Gearóid Ó Tuathail (Gerard Toal), *Critical Geopolitics: The Politics of Writing Global Space*

Volume 5 Roxanne Lynn Doty, *Imperial Encounters: The Politics of Representation in North-South Relations*

Volume 4 Thom Kuehls, *Beyond Sovereign Territory: The Space of Ecopolitics*

Volume 3 Siba N'Zatioula Grovogui, *Sovereigns, Quasi Sovereigns, and Africans: Race and Self-Determination in International Law*

Volume 2 Michael J. Shapiro and Hayward R. Alker, editors, *Challenging Boundaries: Global Flows, Territorial Identities*

Volume 1 William E. Connolly, *The Ethos of Pluralization*

On the Way to Diplomacy

COSTAS M. CONSTANTINOU

BORDERLINES, VOLUME 7

 University of Minnesota Press

Minneapolis

London

Published by the University of Minnesota Press
111 Third Avenue South, Suite 290
Minneapolis, MN 55401-2520
Printed in the United States of America on acid-free paper

Book design by Will Powers
Set in Sabon and Officina types
by Stanton Publication Services, Inc., Saint Paul, Minnesota
Printed on recycled paper (50% recycled / 10% postconsumer)

Library of Congress Cataloging-in-Publication Data

Constantinou, Costas M.
   On the way to diplomacy / Costas M. Constantinou.
      p.   cm. — (Borderlines ; v. 7)
   Includes index.
   ISBN 0-8166-2684-7 (hc). — ISBN 0-8166-2685-5 (pb)
   1. Diplomacy—Philosophy.   2. Diplomacy—History.   I. Title.
II. Series: Borderlines (Minneapolis, Minn.) ; v. 7
JX1635.C66   1993
327.1′01—dc20   96-6310

The University of Minnesota is an equal-opportunity educator and employer.

ordre du jour

toast

For theory is an aboriginal embassy.

preamble

The preamble, *somewhat formal in style, setting out the names of the parties in the agreement, the names of the plenipoten- tiaries and the object of the agreement.*—RALPH FELTHAM, Diplomatic Handbook

In the fictitious world of novels, which is only by convention less real than our own, there is a story about a highly respected and responsible ambassador who is seduced into an undiplomatic affair by a promiscuous young woman who is also the mistress of his third secretary. As a result, a scandal breaks inside the embassy, inquisitive questions are asked from the headquarters, and his family cannot uphold its expected social posture. What is more, this newly embraced way of living radically changes the way the ambassador looks at the diplomatic world he has been accustomed to. He realizes he is an other. His body is regimented by protocol. His acts are always scrutinized, calculated in advance for their implications. His instructions come from a monstrous bureaucratic machine maintained by the sheer momentum of habit. His language is a combination of national myths, diplomatic clichés, and personal illusions. The horrifying emptiness of his work elicits a bitter acknowledgment: *I am just playing a part, that of a voyager, an ambassador, delegated from death into this foreign country*. Still, after everything he believes in has been lost and just before his official demise, a mysterious sense of duty leads him back to the embassy, seats him at the ambassadorial desk to complete—yet again—the diplomatic business of the day. A true actor, it seems, has to die on stage.

Perhaps one should read this story of André Brink's *The Ambassador* not just as a portrayal of professional midlife crisis, nor simply as a narration of fantastic episodes in diplomatic practice. Interestingly, the publication of the novel in 1963 prompted the South African Department of Foreign Affairs to conduct an official inquiry in order to establish the source of possible leaks inside the diplomatic service. As the author found to his astonishment, "Arms negotiations between France and South Africa, which I had used as a fiction because it suited the plot, turned out to have been taking place in reality; a South African ambassador in Europe, as it transpired, had actually been involved in the kind of relationship depicted in the book."[1] This is surely a funny coincidence. But the space it occupies between novelty and actuality merits attention—and possibly another inquiry, this time into the politics of language that write the practice of diplomacy.

On the one hand, and on the basis of this "true" story, one could begin to question both the contemporary ambassadorial part and the modern diplomatic plot. That is to say, how is it that at the end of the twentieth century we are confronted by an important global play, the purpose of which a principal participant may not always find easy to understand, let alone confidently explain to the uninitiated? And how does a supposedly clear plot—the negotiation of sovereign states through official representatives—seem to get mixed up with representations of authority, style, habit, belief, honor, masculinity, morality, desire, solitude, and solidarity, and inevitably with the work of the disciplines that study them? On the other hand, this story brings forth the performative power and value of fiction for critical investigation. In a period when theory's capacity to represent reality has been fundamentally challenged by postpositivist and postempiricist critiques, it seems to me that fiction manages to offer a more modest, yet more honest way of writing than most scholarly inquiries. The novel does not claim to correspond to reality; it does not claim to speak the truth. It is accepted as being in the business of producing realities and true, make-believe situations, though it is also in the business of revealing something about the world we live in. Such power of enactment traditionally reserved for fiction may nonetheless offer an insight into the logotechnic practices of diplomatic theory as well—that is, its words, themes, styles, and metaphors, and their role in the constitution of the diplomatic world they describe and explain. In other words, the generalized art of fiction could evoke an inquiry into how the creative power of theory likewise constructs the very subject matter it purports to study objectively, thus requiring different standards of reading and believing.

In the real world of politics, which is only by convention less fictitious than a novel, there are interestingly numerous stories of literati who came to practice diplomacy (Ivo Andrić, Pablo Neruda, Octavio Paz, George Seferis, and Miloš Tsernianski, among many others). One recent case is that of Václav Havel, who while acting in his official capacity as president of Czechoslovakia addressed an international organization in what could be described, at least, as novel diplomatic language:

> The modern era has been dominated by the culminating belief, expressed in different forms, that the world—and Being as such—is a wholly knowable system governed by a finite number of universal laws that man can grasp and rationally direct for his own benefit. The world today is a world in which generality, objectivity and universality are in crisis. This world presents a great challenge to the practice of politics which, it seems to me, still has a technocratic, utilitarian approach to Being, and therefore to political power as well. . . . It is my impression that sooner or later politics will be faced with the task of finding a new, post-modern face.[2]

Is this writing, then, diplomacy, political theory, or literature? Does the distinction make sense any longer, and does it matter? Can one foreclose the way the diplomatic speaks or will speak? And what if one were to adopt Havel's proposition to test not simply the problem of technical and disciplinarian discourses but language itself as a political problematic? What if this question of language—how it is used, how it means, what it does—is what a postmodern politics involves? Havel transgressively uses diplomatic language to restate the practice of politics by questioning the capability of attending to global problems simply "through technical means . . . through the invention of new organizational, political and diplomatic instruments."[3] It is this technological approach to world politics that I also address by restating theory and diplomacy, focusing on the language that precedes them and works to determine their way.[4] I argue that this incessant rereading and critical rewriting of the path that leads to theory/diplomacy constitutes ways of, and opens up thinking spaces for, practicing politics differently.

Consequently, *On the Way to Diplomacy* reviews the literature of diplomacy by investigating the politics of its language. Specifically, it seeks to rethink the concept of diplomacy by rethinking the concept of theory. It does so in the belief that modern diplomacy—or the so-called dialogue between states—is a historically specific interpretation and a theoretically determined rendition of global communication. To that extent, the book examines the philosophical presuppositions and political implications of conventional theories of diplomacy and subsequently explores *theoria* as a different way of approaching the problematic. *Theoria* exposes the originary, etymological, and philosophical association between theory and diplomacy—in ancient Greece *theoria* meant both philosophical thinking and a solemn or sacred embassy sent to discharge a religious duty and/or to consult the oracle. *Theoria* is therefore both metatheory and theory-as-practice. The structures of diplomacy and theory are integrated in the act of representation that is peculiar to Western metaphysical thought. To employ theoria as the contemplative journey and embassy that it is, is to think about theory and diplomacy not as fixed or primordial terms but as discursively and historically conditioned ones. By considering the effects of making sovereign representations, the book reassesses the way to diplomacy—that is to say, it looks at what is politically at stake in bestowing the diplomatic identity and subsequently working with total theories of it. In the process, the relationship between the diplomacy-theory intertext and etymological, mythological, theological, and artistic texts is investigated. The book also deals with questions of agency, duplicity, framing and staging, community, and communication in world politics.

The way of theoria is not always a journey forward. Schematically expressed it primarily involves two steps backward. If the first step (of theory) is the one through which diplomacy is understood and explained, the second step (of theory) is the one that tries to understand this understanding and explain this explaining. In this sense, this theory of theory is an attempt to rethink what is involved in our attempts to know and practice diplomacy. This is necessary because, as I propose in this book, our understanding of diplomacy has been arrested by the metaphysical categories that are technically employed to do the explaining. To overcome these categories and the confinements of the tradition of Western metaphysical thought, one cannot simply reject them and then declare victory. Contesting this confinement involves, instead, an extensive reading back, an appro-

priation of the history of metaphysics in more originary and resourceful ways. This in turn calls for a process of deconstruction, examining diplomatic theory in its historicity, retrieving the experiences deposited in its elemental words and now concealed or
forgotten. For such elemental words reveal and create (it is politically noteworthy that they do both, and not just one or the other) a
text that is being renewed and redrawn differently in different historical epochs.

But this project is not just a reiteration of or return to the past. By
retrieving concealed and forgotten meanings, not only can we explain in a more satisfactory way the condition of possibility of the
categories currently employed in our attempts to know diplomacy
but also challenge the closure of such categories in terms of their understanding and proper use. This "archaeology of knowledge" or
"history of the present," to use Michel Foucault's terms, is therefore
a device by which we can seek to explain and understand the limited
possibilities of technical knowledge sequestered within our inherited
institutions and contemporary conditions of learning and, by doing
so, also explore new ways of thinking and practicing politics.

To that extent, there is also a futuristic projection in this work.
Although not directly addressing or predicting the future of diplomacy, it submits that a better way of confronting those who herald
the end of diplomacy in an era of multiple global actors, mass media,
and satellite communication is to outflank them theoretically, by
suggesting that diplomacy may not simply consist of that interstate,
intersovereign, and interambassadorial side that they see as an
anachronism. Put differently, the answer to the end-of-diplomacy
proposition should not be simply and simplistically to insist that,
say, the functions of the diplomatic mission as enshrined in Article 3
of the Vienna Convention on Diplomatic Relations (1961) still require the human dimension and professional qualities of the resident
envoy but, rather, to argue that Article 3 is neither exclusive nor exhaustive of the functions, actors, processes of communication,
agents, or objects of diplomacy. Quite contrary to the conventional,
protective tendency to fix meanings and settle definitions, it could be
actually in the interest of diplomacy and those interested in its continued scholarly study and practical relevance not to foreclose the
question of what diplomacy is or to restrict what it should entail. In
short, a less rigid—that is, more novel—diplomatic world, a world

that recognizes movement, contingency, and possibility, is what might be required at this stage to save the real one. Novelizing diplomacy is one way to unbar the restrictive structures and unlock new interpretations of diplomatic practice, in the space of which André Brink's fatal ambassador—now in search of new plays or authors—might just negotiate an escape.

The book begins by examining, through Hans Holbein's painting *"The Ambassadors,"* how the technical representations or world picture of diplomacy produce a frame-up. It is subsequently divided into six parts, different stages or actualizations of theoria. Here, I use the ancient Greek terminology because the Greek discloses better the etymological connection with theoria. These parts pursue (a) *Theoris* (medium, path); (b) *Theoria* (embassy, journey); (c)*Thema* (theme); (d) *Theama* (spectacle); (e) *Theon-ora* (the sight or hour of god); and (f) *Theorema* (theorem). The discourses subsequently included in these parts employ the traditional language of diplomacy to illustrate and reinforce the diplomatic character of theoria.

Theoris forms the first stage of theoria. *Theoris* was the sacred ship and the holy path. It constituted the method of transportation that carried theoria and marked its way. In this part, I examine how contemporary postmetaphysical philosophy offers interpretations of theory through the medium of embassy. Then I move to the second part, *Theoria,* to inquire into the diplomatic theory-practice problematic and recover the etymological, philosophical, and political career of the term *theoria.*

Thema is the third part to follow. *Thema,* for theoria, was the subject matter, the problem taken to the oracle for advice. But in philology *thema* is also known as the concept that deals with the inflectional bases, the modifications and additions to the root of the word. In this part, the history of the word *diplomacy* is investigated, and themes deposited in it are retrieved.

The fourth part, *Theama,* introduces the theatrical aspect of theoria as found in the etymological link and political association with the ancient Greek *theatron.* Spectacle was an important function for the solemn ambassadors sent to participate in religious festivals or to witness the Hellenic games. They had to view and be viewed. They had to engage both as actors and spectators, and so both produced and consumed a spectacle. Such is also the case with modern diplomats. *Theama* is the section that deals, therefore, with the protocol, staging, and performance of diplomacy through a complex economy of regard.

Theon-ora deals with the sight (*ora*) or hour (*hora*) of god (*theon*) in diplomacy, *theon-ora* being the encounter-with-god-in-the-shrine aspect of theoria. Here, I examine how a theological interpretation, though not exclusive, exposes marginal diplomatic sites, like acts of commensality and dietary practices, as forms of communication and modes of creating community.

Theorema concerns the final part of the book. It comes at the end because it was the part that brought theoria to a conclusion. *Theorema* is the word or saying (*rema*) of god (*theos*) that constituted the prophecy, the divine message communicated to the ambassadors. But the ancient Greeks knew only too well, when sending missions to consult the oracle, that the truth of the *theorema* was bound to be equivocal (*diphoroumeni*). For them the purpose of theoria was not so much in the prophecy negotiated through the oracle as in the ritual voyage to the shrine. It was the voyage itself that had already established the truth of the *theorema*. The theoric journey should be seen consequently not as a means but as an end in itself—an end that opens up the possibility for new beginnings.

Before embarking, an acknowledging note is in order. An earlier version of *démarche* was published in *Millennium* 23 (Spring 1994). For comments and critical readings (though unfortunately not for responsibility that remains mine), I am indebted to David Campbell, James Der Derian, Richard Little, Mike Shapiro, Rob Walker, and especially to Mick Dillon for his encouragement and committed involvement. For his hospitality and endurance of my heretic views, my thanks to the president of the Pontifical Ecclesiastic Academy, Archbishop Rauber. On a different front, Sue Wiles patiently assisted with confusing word-processing packages and relieved typing burdens during the final stages. Finally, I would like to acknowledge the unrelenting support of my family and close friends, the importance of which they do not always realize, and frankly without which this project would not have been possible. In this respect, Demey deserves, at least, one last sentence of her own.

démarche

The closest English equivalent for the expression "faire une démarche" *is* "make representations" *but it should be remembered that the word in French covers all manner of representations from proposals to threats.*—SIR HAROLD NICOLSON, Diplomacy

Hans Holbein, *"The Ambassadors,"* reproduced by courtesy of the Trustees of the National Gallery, London

The difference between international politics as it actually is and a rational theory derived from it is like the difference between a photograph and a painted portrait. The photograph shows everything that can be seen by the naked eye; the painted portrait does not show everything that can be seen by the naked eye, but it shows, or at least seeks to show, one thing that the naked eye cannot see: the human essence of the person portrayed. . . . Political realism wants the photographic picture of the political world to resemble as much as possible its painted portrait.—HANS MORGENTHAU, Politics among Nations

This picture ["The Ambassadors"] *is simply what any picture is, a trap for the gaze.*—JACQUES LACAN, The Four Fundamental Concepts of Psycho-Analysis

Diplomatic Representations . . . or Who Framed the Ambassadors?

Hans Holbein's painting *"The Ambassadors"* is a popular one with theorists of diplomacy. In it, diplomacy is traditionally found to be represented in the form of a picture, enclosed and framed for us to see, open to scholarly study and investigation. Consequently, what hangs on the walls of the National Gallery in London is more than just a painting of mere interest to the art critic or historian. As I intend to sketch below, it constitutes a globalized picture of diplomacy, of the representations of diplomacy (the démarches) and of the representatives of diplomacy (the ambassadors).

Even more important, the painting can be taken as a site on which the structure of representation in general, and diplomatic representation in particular, can be opened up and vividly illustrated. This cannot be done, however, in an unqualified didactic manner as if the Holbein painting offers us a legible schooltext that simply awaits reading and learning. Before rushing to see in the picture the acts of diplomatic representation, this introductory chapter has some important questions to ask. Namely, how is it that this painting represents diplomacy? How is it that diplomacy is seen, placed before our very eyes? What are the conditions, in other words, that allow the placing of diplomacy in this picture? And how is a representation of diplomacy distinguished as such? I ask these questions first because they build the path to the core questions of this book. How does diplomatic representation work? What kind of symbolic

3

processes do we encounter on the way to diplomacy? And what do they tell us about the study of diplomatic theory in particular, and the practice of diplomacy in general?

In this chapter, therefore, I examine two issues concerning diplomatic representation and its function, before drawing some conclusions about the contemporary state of diplomacy and its relation to international relations (IR) theory. The first issue examined is how one can indeed find representations of diplomacy in Holbein's painting once the diplomatic frame is adopted—that is to say, how the frame is applied in order to "trap the gaze" and capture the reality of diplomacy. I take as my starting point that reality is not an objective state of being. More specifically, I want to argue that we see the world through representations that frame our experiences and label them as part of reality. The Holbein painting constitutes, in this sense, one such representation of diplomacy. The painting represents diplomacy by giving it a presence in the space of this work of art; the painted presence stands in the place of an absent signified or idea of diplomacy that is supposed to exist and be present elsewhere. Diplomatic representation, to that extent, is not deemed to be "a break in presence" but "a separation and a continuous, homogeneous modification of presence in representation."[1] I examine the application of the diplomatic frame and the representation of diplomacy in Holbein's painting in the first part of this chapter.

In the second part, I move from the specific picture of *"The Ambassadors"* to the more general world picture of diplomacy. Here, I use Martin Heidegger's notion of "enframing" to put forward and develop the point that everyday diplomatic representation engages in framing processes—similar to the ones in the Holbein painting—that work to produce diplomatic reality. In diplomatic representation, I argue, diplomacy is framed for us to see; but in the process we are also framed to see diplomacy. In short, I suggest that one can better understand the contemporary diplomatic framework as a frame-up. In the third part, I draw some concluding thoughts on how the enframing of diplomatic representation can inform contemporary debates in IR theory in general and diplomacy in particular.

But why go to a painting to question diplomatic representation? Why resort to such an apparently marginal case as opposed to more serious, official sites of diplomacy like security, negotiation, power, interest, and so on? I do so for a number of reasons. The first reason is precisely that painting is not deemed an official representation and consequently neglected. If one is to challenge the closure of representation successfully, one must go beyond "the limits of the state," beyond the representation that is authoritatively named the "official": "To pose the problem in terms of the State means to continue posing it in terms of sovereign and sovereignty, that is to say in terms of law."[2] To pose the problem of diplomacy in terms of painting and enframing is, therefore, to examine it outside the traditional forms of posing the problematic.

The second reason relates to how painting prompts one to think explicitly about the issue of the frame, and so also to address the borders or margins within which diplomatic representation is framed. As Michel Foucault showed in his own works on madness, sexuality, illness, and criminality, one can find the same (and often more vividly illustrated) knowledge struggles and interpretive contests applied also to marginal or micropolitical practices. In conventional diplomacy, painting would be considered in terms of decoration or as part of the "dignified"—as opposed to the "effective"—work in diplomacy.[3] Painting offers, therefore, a particularly good case study because it constitutes the limit condition of diplomacy, that is to say, the necessary limits but also the theoretical limitations of its very identity. Equally, its frame addresses the question of inside and outside by marking (and remarking on) the borderlines within which the diplomatic framework is defined and normalized.

The third reason for examining a painting is that it exemplifies the condition of modernity, and so of modern diplomacy, in the most radical and yet most philosophical of ways. A painting is an exemplar of the "world picture" of modernity.[4] More specifically, it can help one understand diplomatic representation in terms of modern representative thinking.[5] Representative thought involves the task of presenting the unpresentable: "Showing that there is something we can conceive of which we can neither see nor show."[6] This form of thinking is a general characteristic of modernity, and so it is of the thinking of modern diplomacy. Diplomacy, as the official medium of sovereign political representations, can be therefore rethought through an exegesis of the structure of the world picture and of modern representative thought.

In sum, this book shifts focus away from the conventional problematic of diplomacy and international relations. It suggests, in contrast, that before examining the question of how we *relate internationally*, we should first examine the question of how we *relate to beings* at all; particularly, in this instance, how we relate to diplomacy as a being-in-the-world and as an instrument for representing and explaining the world.

THE DIPLOMATIC FRAME

Let us now look closely at the Holbein painting and the diplomatic images it presents. This will be done first by examining the various diplomatic readings that have been made of the painting and then by exploring the history of the painting with particular reference to its frame. Subsequently, I intend to address the framing of diplomacy in *"The Ambassadors"* and how this framing also applies more generally to the debates about the possibility of diplomatic theory.

Picturing Diplomacy

In his British Library catalog of diplomatic articles, Peter Barber gives a detailed description of what is pictured, of what we can see in *"The Ambassadors"*:

> This famous canvas was commissioned to commemorate the visit in April 1533 of Georges de Selve, Bishop of Lavaux (1508/9–41) (right) to his friend Jean de Dinteville, Seigneur de Polisy and Bailly de Troyes (1504–55) (left), who was then in London negotiating the truce between England and Scotland on behalf of the King of France. *The diplomatic background of both men accounts for the painting's traditional name.* The room is littered with objects. Though each has symbolic significance, like the distorted skull at the front traditionally serving as a reminder of the shortness of life, *the items indicate the variety of the ambassador's interests.* Among the objects on the top of the stand against which de Dinteville and de Selve lean are a globe of the heavens, a portable cylindrical sundial, seeming to show the date of 11th April, and another polyhedral sundial. On the lower shelf there is a lute with a broken string, an open hymnal, with music to Luther's version of *Veni Creator Spiritus* and the Ten Commandments, a half-open book of arithmetic and a globe onto which Holbein has painted geographical features including the name of de Dinteville's home, Polisy, where this picture was to be seen until 1653. Half-hidden by the curtain at the top left-hand corner is a crucifix. *Diplomatic theorists through the ages have always stressed the*

*ambassador's need for versatility and would, no doubt, have ap-
plauded this display of it.*[7]

Observing diplomacy as painted in art, Barber's reading of Holbein's painting is important. This is particularly so because it points to the array of objects in the picture to indicate specific areas of diplomatic interest and practice (such as the need for versatility). Furthermore, the marked contrast in the outfit of the portrayed ("splendid clothes" of the one compared with the "sombre, clerical attire" of the other) prompts Barber to engage in an interesting analysis of the impact of ecclesiastical diplomacy on modern diplomatic practices.[8]

Similarly the painting is pictured on the front cover of James Der Derian's book *On Diplomacy*. The jacket illustration reads more or less the same:

> A detail from *Jean de Dinteville and Georges de Selve ("The Ambas-
> sadors")*, 1533, by Hans Holbein is reproduced by courtesy of the
> Trustees, National Gallery, London. The items signal the variety of
> the Ambassadors' interests: a globe of the heavens, two sundials, a
> lute with a broken string, an open hymnal, a book of arithmetic and a
> globe with geographical features painted on.[9]

Indirectly, Barber's picturing of diplomacy has also been applauded by a more traditional scholar. In criticizing Der Derian's representations of diplomacy, Christopher Hill also turns to Barber's collection of diplomatic articles: "For the wider ramifications of diplomacy, we shall still want to turn to . . . Peter Barber's delightful catalogue for the British Library's 1979 exhibition on the history of diplomacy."[10]

In another instance, John Carroll reads Holbein's double portrait as an epitome of humanism. Here, the ambassadors figure as "two exemplars of the Renaissance":

> They are men of great eminence in the secular and clerical worlds.
> They have wealth, power and high office, both by birth and appoint-
> ment. They have the trust of their king, François I. They are also men
> of learning, with all the symbols of humanist culture at their com-
> mand. Their dress, their relaxed stance, their sober gaze straight out
> of the painting, tell of their authority. They are masters of their
> world. *They are more than ambassadors of France, they are emis-
> saries of Humanism.* They are the worthy heirs of the Gattamelata,
> the noble gentleman on whose shoulders the success of the new cul-
> ture rests. . . . The ambassadors are not only learned, they are free.

They enjoy free-will. They move about the civilized world using their power to organize the possibilities of men; the fate of Kingdoms is in their hands.[11]

Finally, Linda and Marsha Frey on examining attitudes toward diplomatic immunity during the sixteenth century suggest in passing that "the Ambassadors—Holbein's celebrated tableau bestows a dignity of status not always guaranteed by those who encountered the envoy."[12]

What if diplomacy is painted? In a way, there is nothing wrong with reading diplomacy or details of the ambassadors' interests and status in a painting; Barber, Der Derian, Hill, Carroll, and the Freys are all entitled to do so. Setting aside the Platonic downgrading of art—that is, as a mere imitation of reality—there is a good case to be made for the discovery of a representation of diplomacy in a painting.[13] Painters are writers of a kind; they draw, they write in forms and colors, they are *zoo-graphoi* (writers of life). On the other hand, writing itself involves, just like painting, the graphic production of images. It deals with the imageological because writing always points to another picture, to a signified beyond the here and now. One can then find representations of diplomacy, as with the rhetoric of language, in the aesthetics of the picture and in the pictorial truth it brings into being. After all, if a picture is called *"The Ambassadors,"* one can reasonably look there for something diplomatic. The title alone entitles it.

A Short History of the Frame

But what if *"The Ambassadors"* proves to be a bluff, as certain art historians have already suggested? What if the frame of its representation is a frame-up? What are we then to make of these apparent diplomatic readings? In answering these questions, we find that the frame becomes both interesting and important. This is because the disputed identity of the painting, and the question of naming it *"The Ambassadors,"* was finally resolved over a detail concerning its frame. The frame was the most significant factor, for it established the coincidence of *the* painting now exhibited in the National Gallery in London with *a* certain painting (possibly painted by Holbein) that portrayed Jean de Dinteville and Georges de Selve. In short, there was historical evidence that the latter was actually painted in 1532 or 1533, but there was no evidence (no writing, label, or title) to link that painting with the one possessed by the National Gallery. The link was to be found in the frame and in the framing process.

The history of the painting is a long and disputed one. To deal with all readings of and exhaust all historical references to *"The Ambassadors"* would require a book in itself. The painting is a semiotician's paradise as much as it is a historiographer's maze. I will, therefore, confine myself as much as possible to my diplomatic concerns.

The first point to note is that the painting was never named by Holbein but acquired its name later (when taken as the double portrait of two ambassadors). I am interested in how the painting acquired its name (also the identities of the portrayed) because once the identity of the picture becomes established as *"The Ambassadors,"* the diplomatic reading of it follows naturally.

In the late nineteenth and early twentieth centuries, when most of the discussions regarding the painting's identity took place, there were a number of different interpretations concerning the persons portrayed.[14] In this period of identity crisis, the painting was also referred to as *"The Scholars"* or *"The Poets."* At that time, suggestions as to who the portrayed persons were varied. Ralph Wornum and Alfred Woltmann (the nineteenth-century leading authorities on Holbein) argued that it was a painting of the poet Sir Thomas Wyatt with his friend Leland. Sidney Colvin claimed that the second figure was the poet Nicholas Bourbon, and William Dickes argued that it was a painting of the German palatines, Otto Henry and Philip.[15]

In fact, in 1890 when the painting was purchased by the National Gallery, little was known about its history apart from a recorded entry in *Galerie des Peintres Flammands, Hollandais et Allemands* published in 1792 by Jean Batiste Pierre Le Brun, who was known once to have had the painting in his possession. In what appeared to be a laconic and "a very bad engraving" (in Mary Hervey's words), Le Brun mentions a picture of two ambassadors, de Selve and d'Avaux. It was simply, and only, because of this single piece of information that the picture acquired the title *"The Ambassadors."*

Le Brun's identification was, however, flawed on five grounds. First, d'Avaux, one of the ambassadors allegedly portrayed in the painting, was found to have lived at least a hundred years after the picture was painted. Second, the dimensions of the painting as given by Le Brun were different from those of the painting in the National Gallery. Third, Le Brun stated that there had been no date or signature on the picture, whereas the National Gallery possession was dated (1533) and signed by Ioannes Holbein Pingebat. Fourth, he provided no information as to how the painting was acquired. Fifth, Le Brun offered no general description of the painting that he named, thus making it impossible to associate it with the one possessed by the National Gallery.

But the most astonishing fact of all these revelations was that they did nothing to change the painting's title as *"The Ambassadors."* For by the time the National Gallery had acquired it, the diplomatic title had obtained such permanency for the faithful that the conflicts surrounding it were conveniently ignored. The inconvenient contradictions were dismissed as "excessive carelessness on the part of French writers [which] is probably the main explanation of the discrepancies."[16] But, at the same time, it should be remembered, this "carelessness" of the French writers accounted for the diplomatic identity of the picture in the first place.

In her massive historical study of *"The Ambassadors,"* Mary Hervey shows how the diplomatic identity of the painting was always taken for granted, being simply a matter of gathering the necessary "information which had so long been sought in vain" (11); "such was the state of things when, in 1895, a fortunate discovery came to confirm the probabilities thus evolved, and to raise them to the certainty of fact" (10).

The story of the acquisition of evidence is interesting in itself. The "fortunate discovery" for Hervey followed the publication of *Revue de champagne et de brie* (1888), which led Hervey (after seven years of painful research) to M. Saffroy, an antiquarian bookseller of Pré-Saint-Gervais, who actually possessed an old manuscript (label). That manuscript named a picture of two ambassadors, de Dinteville and de Selve, painted by a Dutch painter in England in 1532 or 1533, later kept in Polisy. The fact that the manuscript consisted "of an oblong piece of parchment which may have been cut at some time from an inventory" led Hervey and the National Gallery experts to the conclusion that this was part of the frame of *the* painting: "It seems possible that it was attached to the painting as a label in the early days of its next sojourn" (12).

Two questions follow these assumptions. Was this manuscript really part of a frame? And if it was part of *a* frame, was it part of *the* frame? Although Hervey does well in the beginning to qualify the result of this discovery—"if fastened to the frame"—she later takes this for granted: "The date of the document is in accordance with this supposition. On submission to the authorities at the British Museum, its authenticity was pronounced to be indisputable" (12). How the date of the document and its verified authenticity "proved" that everything was "in accordance with this supposition," namely that the label was actually *"fastened to the* frame," remains a mystery. And does this raise the probabilities to the certainty of fact? We can speculate, but can we really know? One can notice further wishful thinking by Hervey when she concludes that the manuscript now "appears early to have become separated from the picture and its proprietors, and to have fallen into careful hands" (12). Note that these are now "careful" French hands. Finally, observe the climax and the happy conclusion of the story: "The identity of the 'Ambassadors' was now fully established" (13).

Consequently, the presupposition that the discovered manuscript was fastened to the frame, taken as part of the frame, then for some time lost and later discovered appears to be the determining detail (the "indisputable" proof) for the identity and title of the painting. Because of this information, the painting was finally nailed to a diplomatic frame and associated with diplomacy. It should be noted, however, that the label offered no description at all of the painting or the persons portrayed (other than their names and missions), but simply that these two "historical" persons were actually painted in England, in 1532 or 1533, by "an excellent Dutch painter."[17]

What then is the effect if the persons portrayed in *"The Ambassadors"* are not really ambassadors? Have we been framed to read diplomacy in this picture? Another extensive historical study of the painting claims precisely this. In his historical investigation, Dickes finds that the persons portrayed are not ambassadors but counts palatine, Otto Henry the Magnanimous and Philip, Defender of Vienna, the painting being a memorial of the Treaty of Nuremberg (1532).[18] He puts his case in an open letter:

To the Trustees and Director of the National Gallery,

Gentlemen,
    Impressed with the historical importance of Holbein's picture, the so called "AMBASSADORS," I venture again to lay before you the result of my studies. This I do in the belief that you can hardly be satis-

fied with the statement on the suppositious parchment label, that the persons represented are "Messire Jean de D'Inteville" (the invalid French Ambassador Jean Dinteville) and "Messire George de Selve, Evesque de Lavaur," and that you will not be unwilling to consider what the picture has to say.

I have the honour to remain

Your obedient Servant[19]

Note that Dickes also refers to "the suppositious parchment label" and regards the issue of whether it was part of the picture's frame as the determining factor, the one that finally led the trustees to retain the title of *"The Ambassadors."*[20] Dickes offers a different explanation as to the naming of the painting. He argues that because the picture had hung in M. Beaujon's palace, it was only natural to gain the reputation of representing ambassadors, for "that house was also known as *l'Hotel Ambassadeurs Extraordinaires"* (10). There was also a commercial interest in giving the painting such a dignified title: "The concealed vendor who put it in the Beaujon sale, knowing that large portraits of aliens were unsaleable, sought to give it the prestige of belonging to the 'Hotel des Ambassadeurs' and secure for it patriotic regard, by appropriating the names of two famous French diplomats" (11).

Despite Dickes's revelations, however, there has been no shift in the viewpoint of the National Gallery. There are, of course, some official acknowledgments concerning the painting's identity. The title is often put in quotation marks mainly to signify that this is not the painter's title. Moreover, the entry in *The National Gallery Collection* makes some additional qualifications about the name: "Apt and well-established as is the popular title of this painting, it is not strictly correct."[21] Note, however, that this refers not to the identity of the portrayed as ambassadors but to the fact that "the two men shown . . . never served as ambassadors together" (126). The National Gallery entry still suggests that visitors regard the painting as the double portrait of two men who both served as ambassadors, albeit in different historical periods. In short, as far as the National Gallery is concerned, the ambassadorial status of the two men portrayed remains intact.

For our purposes, we must repeat that the question whether this picture represents the ambassadors and their interests depends, in turn, on whether an old parchment label was part of the frame of this picture. That is the matter that gives this picture a diplomatic frame. This makes it of interest to diplomacy and allows a reading of diplomacy in the picture. Even if, for the sake of argument, the figures in the painting were ambassadors, there is no evidence that Holbein intended to paint "the wider ramifications of diplomacy" in this picture. Instead, he could have merely scattered a number of different articles of interest to theologians or literati of the period around his models either to gain a higher fee or simply for fun.[22] And even if he intended that we see diplomacy in his picture, this is not enough to make it visible unless, again, the diplomatic frame is adopted. For the reading of *"The Ambassadors"* as representing ambassadors and of the articles as representing objects of their interest results after the repression of all the other potential identities the two persons and the articles could have had. In sum, in Holbein's painting diplomacy has been framed for us to see, and we have been framed in seeing diplomacy.

Framing Diplomacy

By adopting the diplomatic frame, one can read all the items in the painting as diplomatic ones, as items representative of the acts of diplomacy. One is now attuned to see diplomacy because the frame has established a homology. Reading pregnant details and developing specific allusions from a diplomatic perspective can easily follow.

Thus the painting can be viewed as an "ambitious work [that] alludes to the preoccupations of the two diplomats it portrays."[23] The "complex double portrait" can "admirably stand for state and church."[24] It could be taken to be celebrating the experiences of the French ambassador at the court of Henry VIII and the "diplomatic and moral support" offered by his visiting friend.[25] On the surface the painting appears to allude to a "confident" (secularized?) diplomatic world, but on closer examination it could be found to be full of "references to religious divisions of the day."[26] This tension in diplomatic practice is perhaps further signified through the arrangement of the objects; the objects on the upper shelf are "for understanding the heavens," whereas those on the lower shelf can signify "educated pursuits of the earthly realm."[27] Luther's translation of *Veni Creator Spiritus* could refer to the emerging role of Protestantism in diplomatic affairs or perhaps "present an appeal for spiritual guidance in resolving the nation's religious and diplomatic tangles."[28] The half-concealed crucifix, however, could allude also to the diminishing value of religious influence in diplomacy. The terrestrial globe can point out the impact of the discovery of the new world (globalization of diplomacy, though still fundamentally Eurocentric) and the freeing of heavenly authority through the Copernican revolution. This aspect could also be seen in the celestial globe, which could be interpreted to mean mastery over the heavens; the sundials, the quadrant and the *apians torqutum* are instruments by which heaven comes under human calculation and the realm of science.[29] Similarly, the geometrical instruments and the book of arithmetic could symbolize the emerging scientific interest in diplomacy (arithmetic as one of the seven liberal arts) and the scientific approach to its practice: "Reason and free-will, they are powerful tools, and mankind has benefited prodigiously from their exercise by these ambassadors and their progeny. As long as de Dinteville and de Selve are absorbed in their science, as long as they keep on the move in their diplomacy, all is well."[30] The Order of St. Michael can signify the employment of knights, or nobility in general, in the diplomatic profession. The cap badge can "underline the power and seriousness of the two men's mission."[31] The objects of fine art arranged on the table ("a host of musical instruments and other objects expressive doubtless of their tastes")[32] such as the lute and flutes, can express the cultural influences of diplomacy, in terms of *civilité*, and the practical significance of music and dancing in court.[33] The Renaissance encyclopedia in the painting can point to the understanding of ambassadors as learned individuals and the grounding of diplomatic practice in a good classical background and pansophism. The floor mosaics (derived from the Cosmati work in Westminster Abbey)[34] could signify the importance of court architectonics and décor or perhaps "nationalism and religion effectively combined."[35] The knotted rug can show "cosmopolitan taste and the wealth to indulge it."[36] The individuals' clothes, or more specifically "the green backdrop and the pink slashed shirt of the diplomat [that] add a zest," could signify the ambassador's material enjoyments and gusto.[37] This is just a sample of all the diplomatic readings now made possible by the naming of the picture as *"The Ambassadors."*

The most curious object of all, the one that lies in the foreground of the painting and is most discussed, also plays with and problematizes this entire question of framing, perspective, and seeing. It escapes the first viewing of the picture and appears with the second look, in *anamorphosis*. By means of an artistic trick, what appears in the first instance to be some kind of floating cylinder or cuttlebone, reappears (when seen from a different perspective) to be a skull. Viewers can go through this cycle of perspectival illusion as they walk toward and away from the painting.

What can this mean? What did the artist intend? And what are we to make of this trick that is being deliberately played on our sense of sight? Is it a trick that is inevitably also played on our "sight of sense," the way in which we have been positioned to make sense of the painting as a representation of diplomacy? Can this perspectival trick also put diplomacy into perspective? Does it refer to the double eyeing (*diplo-matia*) or duplicity of diplomacy? Is the feature put there in the painting to serve as a "perpetual hallmark," as the National Gallery catalog integrates it, as a *"memento mori"*? Has the artist painted the skull to point to the ambassadors' "limit of limits"?[38] Does this signify the human *"vanitas"* reminding us of "death and the futility of secular achievement"?[39] Is it true that "these sentiments could also apply to *The Ambassadors*"?[40] And is this also somehow supposed to refer to the tasks of diplomacy? Is this memory of death supposed to invoke a deadly vision of diplomacy, or an all-too-fatal representation of diplomacy? Could it stand as the "one last curse" of the painting, referring to the impossibility of escaping "the eyes of the ambassadors," the "dead stare" of these "emissaries of death"?[41] Or is it the case that "death in *The Ambassadors* has none of the succoring gravity of Ecclesiastes"?[42] Does it point then toward "the end," can it be taken to be a futuristic sign of "the end of diplomacy"? Eventually, who is it that draws the border, the new frame, to decide where this reading of diplomacy ought to stop?

The Frame of Theory

The diplomatic representations of Holbein's painting seem to follow the adoption of the diplomatic frame. The frame itself is what licenses the diplomatic reading of the painting. But the protocols of this framing, as described above, also paint an excellent picture of the framed representation of diplomacy. How can one begin to speak about representation? First of all, where does the frame of it lie? Is it the conventional frame, that which frames the whole picture, that which distinguishes the work of art from the physical environment?

Or is there also an internal frame, one that emphasizes and points to the diplomatic details, distinct but also part of the main representation? Or is it, finally, a more general, abstract frame, one that includes the authorship and the historical context and circumstance of the painting? In short, at which point is the reading of diplomacy in the picture marked, limited, figured, and identified?

One can begin by saying that it is the frame itself that frames *"The Ambassadors,"* not only in the literal sense by establishing the physical boundaries of this work of art, but also in the way that it delimits the parameters of diplomatic representation and subsequently those of diplomatic theory. Jacques Derrida's work on painting, for example, points precisely to this interplay of frame delimitations in our desire to see (and theorize) with the lack of what cannot be seen (and is impossible to theorize): "What does the lack depend on? What lack is it? And what if it were the frame. What if the lack formed the frame of the theory. Not its accident but its frame. More or less still: what if the lack were not only the lack of a theory of the frame but the place of the lack in a theory of the frame."[43]

The study of the Holbein painting in general and of its frame in particular stands for a theory of diplomacy. The conclusion it paints for us is that lack (the absence of diplomacy) forms the frame of theory required to trap the presence of diplomacy. It is a framed view, a spatially bounded presence that in turn inaugurates and justifies a system of sovereign representations. It is important to note at this point that the frame is not merely the edge, the marking of an end, the separation of the internal from the external, the limit that distinguishes the work of art from the artless environment. The frame is constitutive of art and of the representations of art, and so it is of diplomacy. In its inclusion and exclusion processes, in its "arbitrary and barbaric nature of the cutting-out,"[44] the act of framing is exemplary of the theoretical act itself. In other words, the frame is part and parcel of modern theorizing. To follow William E. Connolly, the distinctive characteristic of modern theoretical debates is that they are all framed: "We think restlessly within familiar frameworks to avoid thought about how our thinking is framed. Perhaps that is the ground of *modern* thoughtlessness."[45] In this instance, therefore, by attending to the framing of the picture, the theory of diplomacy can be rethought.

In Holbein's painting, diplomacy is framed, but we are also

framed to see it. In the framing process our gaze is trapped. Diplomacy is given a presence in a captured image as in a calligramme, restituted in pointing, in an infinite play of appearance and disappearance. As shown in the readings of this particular painting, the view of diplomacy is constituted in the frame of theory: the theoretical frame that names and differentiates the diplomatic from the nondiplomatic. By posing the question of the frame, by theorizing the frame, we also subsequently question the representation of diplomacy.

THE DIPLOMATIC FRAMEWORK

In view of the above analysis, I argue that this framing process of *"The Ambassadors"* can also give us an insight into the more general, constitutive processes of the modern diplomatic framework (that is, of the boundaries within which modern diplomacy is practiced and theorized). To that extent, I suggest that the real, everyday representations of diplomacy have the status of the diplomatic representations encountered in the Holbein painting. The contemporary diplomatic framework can be better understood as a frame-up. Diplomacy can be subsequently approached as a "world picture" within which ambassadors are enframed.

Enframing and the Modern World Picture

As mentioned in the beginning of this chapter, Holbein's picture, far from being simply an interesting illustration of the picturing and framing of diplomacy, is also characteristic of the modern condition of representative thinking that ambassadors have to face and work with. Paintings and pictures exemplify representative thinking, not only as simple metaphors of pictorial substitution in the play of presence and absence, but also in a more philosophical manner that is tied to the wider criticism leveled at metaphysical theorizing: namely, that in thinking beyond the physical it forgets the very ground on which its fundamental assumptions are based.

On this point I follow Martin Heidegger who argues that the important question of reflection in the modern age fundamentally concerns the modern "world picture" (*Weltbild*).[46] *World picture* as a term for Being (that which in the history of metaphysics accounts for beings rather than nothing) is not something that existed before René Descartes but, rather, is peculiar to the modern age: "The world picture does not change from an earlier medieval one into a modern one, but rather the fact that the world becomes picture at all is what distinguishes the essence of modern age" (130). Heidegger's argument that the modern man conceives of the world as a picture stems from a reading of the Cartesian thesis that posits man as capable of producing sovereign representations. With Descartes, man becomes a subject (*subiectum*) distinguished from objects and separated from his environment. The Latin word *subiectum* is a translation of the Greek word *hypokeimenon,* which means that which lies before one, as gathering ground (*legein*). With Heidegger, "the world picture would be a painting so to speak, of what is as a whole," a picture placed before the thinking subject as "standing reserve" (*bestand*; 129). In other words, "where the world becomes picture, what is, in its entirety, is juxtaposed as that for which man is prepared and which, correspondingly, he therefore intends to bring before himself and have before himself, and consequently intends in a decisive sense to set in place before himself" (129). As a fixed relational center, the Cartesian man stands before a picture brought forth into presence through his logos, through the language that gathers together and reveals that which lies before. Metaphysical thought and understanding becomes a matter of "getting the picture" and of "getting into the picture." In short, entering the world picture means that man can objectify the world and confidently treat beings as "present at hand."

According to Heidegger, modern man is enframed (*gestell*) in the metaphysical picture that represents him, the very picture that also makes his modern representations possible.[47] Enframing, then, stands precisely for the modern, technologized production of the real.[48] Through enframing, however, the real is not revealed in a simple, natural sense but challenged forth. That is to say, the frame imposes a mode of ordering through which the real is made to stand there as standing reserve. Such enframing works because it "entraps the truth of its own coming to presence with oblivion."[49] Once the real is revealed, the process, the *techne* of enframing that made it possible is forgotten. Once the subject gets the picture and is attuned to it, the frame is marginalized and drifts into oblivion:

> Because we no longer encounter what is called the frame within the purview of representation which lets us think the Being of beings as

presence—the frame no longer concerns us as something that is present—therefore the frame seems at first strange. It remains strange above all because it is not an ultimate, but rather first gives us That which prevails throughout the constellation of Being and man.[50]

Grounded in the picture and forgetting the frame that made the picture possible, man as subject is consequently subjected to the enclosed representations of it. This metaphysical forgetfulness constitutes for Heidegger the "supreme danger" of the modern age because it results in thinking under the illusion of a given and unproblematic presence, that is to say, it conceals the extent to which man is claimed by enframing. The Heideggerian turning and the task of overcoming metaphysics is precisely the deconstruction of the modern picture, the getting out of its enframing.[51]

The Frame-up

What follows from the Heideggerian thesis is that the contemporary world picture of diplomacy appears fully to replicate the enframed representations of the Holbein painting. One is therefore equally enframed in the real, everyday representations of diplomacy. Quite simply, one needs to get into the diplomatic picture if one is to understand diplomacy at all and to be in line and at ease with modern diplomatic theory and practice.

The Holbein picture stands for the imaged embodiment of the seeking of diplomacy. It is an artistic space featuring the adventure of identity. As Jacques Lacan explains in an interesting psychoanalytical study of *"The Ambassadors,"* the apprehension of a world is not a simple question of the perceiving eye; it always involves, rather, the "eye of desire," the eye that seeks the entity and establishes the identity:

> If one does not stress the dialectic of desire one does not understand why the gaze of others should disorganize the field of perception. It is because the subject in question is not that of reflexive consciousness, but that of desire. One thinks it is a question of the geometral eye-point, whereas it is a question of a quite different eye—that which flies in the foreground of *The Ambassadors.*[52]

Apprehending diplomacy in Holbein's painting, therefore, is only the result of the diplomatic eye, the double eye. Diplomacy can never be seen by the pure gaze. The diplomatic eye is always sent on a journey in search of the same entity (id-entity).[53] The diplomatic eye finds diplomacy, but it is also trapped in the closure of the enframed representation. Apprehending diplomacy is the result of a desire that is itself based on lack: the lack of diplomacy, a diplomacy that does not exist and still has to be challenged and framed to appear. Painting diplomacy on a canvas or writing diplomacy in an essay is consequently nothing more than the blind representation of diplomacy's invisible condition of possibility, or put differently, the presence of its perpetual absence.[54]

Diplomacy is put before one as a pregiven representation, as a drawn and redrawn picture. Thus the world becomes a canvas, a *heterotopia* on which diplomacy appears. And language assumes the role of the frame. As Foucault argues:

> The relation of language to painting is an infinite relation. It is not that words are imperfect, or that, when confronted by the visible, they prove insuperably inadequate. Neither can be reduced to the other's terms: *it is in vain that we say what we see; what we see never resides in what we say.* And it is in vain that we attempt to show, by the use of images, metaphors, or similes, what we are saying; the space where they achieve their splendour is not that deployed by our eyes but that defined by the sequential elements of syntax. And the proper name, in this context, is merely an artifice: *it gives us a finger to point with, in other words, to pass surreptitiously from the space where one speaks to the space where one looks; in other words, to fold one over the other as if they were equivalents.*[55]

Foucault refers to the relation between language and painting in the act of naming. Such a relation is also characteristic of the picture of diplomacy, which in its logos appears to be a logical one. Naming a painting *"The Ambassadors,"* for example, allows the scholar to point to the "wider ramifications of diplomacy." The picture the scholar points to, however, is an artifice. For Foucault also specifically challenges the naturalized products of representative thought by offering a distinction between resemblance and similitude. Resemblance is dominated by representation and "presumes a primary reference that prescribes and classes," a faith in an original entity that is supposed to be present elsewhere. Similitude, on the other hand, works on repetition, breaks reference with an "anchor," rejects the "model" and gives no privileged status to an original entity: "Similitude circulates the simulacrum as the indefinite and reversible relation of the similar to the similar."[56] In similitude there is no longer a model picture that determines drawing; neither is there a task for finding an original entity through which to measure identities and the resemblance of their representations.

My point, then, is simply this: diplomacy, like its painting, is similitude. Just like Holbein's painting, the representations of diplomacy appear before us—all of us who currently engage in diplomatic representations and are, as I argue below, ambassadors—not in resemblance but in similitude. The representative view—the enframing—depends on a series of historical repetitions that establish the thing as identifiable, recognizable. Through gaze and oneiric vision, or what Maurice Merleau-Ponty refers to as the sources of apprehension concerning restoration and reconstitution, a totalizing view, an image, a representation of diplomacy can emerge. The representation as produced in the function of "seeingness" or voyeurism renders diplomacy omnipresent and omnivoyant, a privileged object in an otherwise suspended visible/invisible domain—visible if the diplomatic frame is adopted, invisible if not.

It is in the end nothing uncommon, and in a sense not an unconventional point of view, to argue that diplomatic representation functions through simulation, for simulation is traditionally also the art of diplomacy. Simulation is an art, a technique that involves a secret and a challenge. The secret is that diplomacy does not exist. The challenge is to make diplomacy appear. In diplomatic representation, consequently, there is an ironic and fatal alliance, an inaugural quid pro quo between all the subjects involved in the frame-up, that is, the ambassadors (practitioners and theorists) and the subject of diplomacy:

> The practitioner's quid to diplomacy: I will practice you only if you appear.
>
> The theorist's quid to diplomacy: I will study you only if you appear.
>
> Diplomacy's quod to them: I will appear only if you practice and study me.

The reality of these diplomatic representations is, therefore, self-referential. It is based on metaphysical rationality that produces its own closure. It involves the capacity to produce a metaphysical picture, to paint articulations, and to frame presences and absences.

Diplomacy as an artifact is founded precisely on such creative articulations and simulated practices. In forgetting the artistic (what amounts to the Heideggerian forgetfulness of Being), however, the artifact is taken for fact. It is precisely in addressing this circular logic of the artistic that one can begin to enter the logic of the frame-up, and perhaps also to understand the works and arts of diplomacy.[57]

Ambassadors and Their Service

Modern ambassadors are trained to make present the unpresentable and to see what cannot be seen. They are trained to get the picture and to get into the picture. That is why ambassadors are enframed, worked in similar ways to those of *"The Ambassadors."*

Ambassadors are part of, and responsible for, the diplomatic frame-up—the very construction and animation of the diplomatic world they live in. In and through their confident diplomatic representations, ambassadors normalize the frame-up as the framework. Working within this so-called normal framework, they are claimed by their representations and so enter into a power relationship, a relationship of discursive and historical servitude. (Note that the word *ambassador* stems from the Latin word *ambactus*, meaning servant.) Consequently, in their signs and significations, ambassadors effectively become the high servants of this parallel, extraordinary diplomatic service, one that works alongside (and indeed is required to work alongside) the conventional one. Remaining faithful and true to this service means that the frame-up is the only world that ambassadors sense and will ever know. For this world seems the only one that is possible, the only one that makes sense: an enclosed, empty, but at the same time, meaningful world of signs.[58]

The primary role of this incredible service is to make credible representations. For diplomatic representation always involves an act of faith (in the picture). It needs to be accredited. Just as ambassadors are required to present their credentials before they can represent, diplomatic representation also needs to be credited itself with establishing a sovereign presence. This faith in ambassadorial representations and in the presence they establish appears to be a prerequisite for the theory and practice of modern diplomacy, but it is also what nails ambassadors to the frame. It was perhaps symbolic of things to come with the rise of modern diplomacy that in 1462 Duke Fran-

DIPLOMATIC REPRESENTATIONS · 23

cesco Sforza of Milan asked his resident ambassador in Florence to send him three dozen eyeglasses to aggrandize the diplomatic spectacle of his court by framing its members.[59] There is an interesting comparison that can be made here in respect of contemporary ambassadors who in their training and credentials are also equipped with diplomatic frames through which to view, and present views on, the world picture of diplomacy. Ambassadors observe and serve the diplomatic picture; they are both its servants and observants.[60] In the end, what the frame establishes is not only the production of diplomatic reality or presence but also this very service, this faith in the possibility of its representation and technological reproduction.

DIPLOMACY, REPRESENTATION, AND IR THEORY

So far I have proposed that the diplomatic framework is a frame-up. But the modern diplomatic framework is only part of the wider picture and framework of international relations. Is traditional IR theory then equally enframed? And is there a way out of this enframing? The answer to both questions is yes.

Take, for example, the rigid framework of the so-called realist school (and its variations, neorealism, structural realism, and the English school or international society approach) that takes diplomacy as a given representation of interstate relations by which one is expected to abide. There is one important thing to remember about the realist school—namely, that it has nothing to do with the real! By defining itself exclusively in terms of reality and by attaining that reality by enunciation alone, it closes and avoids precisely the question of the real. The more recent developments of the realist school (despite some excellent attempts to reconcile theoretical approaches from neorealism to structural realism) merely achieved the transfer of reality from the referent (the so-called real world out there) to the signified (the realm of ideas).[61] The realists exclude all representations that are not the product of a sovereign political authority. They are schooled to see only certain representations as the ones that really matter. Thus, they are able to pursue epistemological questions assuming that the ontological ones have been resolved.

But the realist framework prompts additional questions that remain unanswered: Why and how do certain representations become dominant? Why and how are certain representations bestowed with an overriding ethical significance? Why and how is truth simply what corresponds with these representations? Why and how are these representations the only ones worthy of the mediation of diplomacy and practice of world politics?

The challenge to the realist school presented by the pluralist approach of Robert Keohane and Joseph Nye amounts merely to a change in perspective. The authors of *Power and Interdependence* still felt the need to fit their theory into the "larger framework of world politics if [they] were to complete the analytical task that [they] had begun."[62] Although Keohane and Nye directly address the rigidity of the realist framework of analysis, questions on how the picture of world politics comes into existence in the first place are again not on the agenda.

Some notable attempts to address the questions raised above, however, and to move the debate further have been pursued by scholars working within the ambit of the Frankfurt School (mainly with the social and political theory of Jürgen Habermas). This has been done even to the extent that critical theory has been announced as the next stage in IR theory.[63] Although the advent of critical theory to the IR discipline is a serious development and one that deserves attention, it seems to me that critical theorists are still not immune to their theoretical framing. It is true that in combining normative, sociological, and praxeological questions the critical theory approach does accommodate a plurality of perspectives and viewpoints, but at the end of the exercise it restricts them by placing them within "a more comprehensive conceptual framework."[64] As Andrew Linklater states, "Moving back and forth between the critical-theoretical framework and individual perspectives is the next stage which needs to be undertaken to develop this project further. The research framework outlined above would then be modified as each perspective was considered in turn" (97–98). To that extent, critical theory appears still to be in search of a critical distance or ideal perspective from which to view and review the picture of world politics. The task of IR theory becomes, consequently, an issue of adjusting and readjusting oneself to the framework. At the end of its theoretical quest, critical theory will still present us with a privileged viewpoint of world politics and ask for subscriptions.

But there have been some other voices in IR theory that in different ways address the question of theoretical framing and its effects on world politics.[65] Without wishing to brush over the differences between these works, I think there are two senses in which their approach is unified. First, they all pay special attention to the issue of the frame by addressing the framed condition of theoretical debates. They do that particularly by examining marginal sites in world politics, that is to say, by attending to the limit condition of identities (the limits within which these identities are defined and so their subsequent theoretical limitations). They also seek to deconstruct the traditional IR framework by uncovering the assumptions and artificial construction of political identities and, in the end, by asking to see the credentials of those who accredit the sovereign presences of these identities.[66] Second, they all resist temptations to offer a final theoretical viewpoint from which the picture of world politics could be explained and understood once and for all. Instead, they suggest a constant opening up of "thinking space" and a celebration of the plurality of views and perspectives.[67] In other words, they take world politics to be an "essentially contested picture." As far as diplomacy is concerned, this approach has been particularly well illustrated in the most recent work of James Der Derian, which proposes that the "diplomacy of late modernity exceeds the representational capabilities of traditional international relations theory."[68]

Where does this leave diplomacy? And how is it to be approached? First, and contrary to the popular belief concerning the intentions of critical approaches, the point of this exercise is not to destroy the picture of diplomacy. It is, rather, to open up the picture to closer examination, particularly how it comes into being and what its effects are. This approach does not take diplomacy as a sovereign presence but examines the whole process of making it present. Put differently, it watches over the whole process of sketching, drawing, painting, and framing, until the picture of diplomacy is hung on the wall as a work of art.

For diplomacy is not just a functional or structural process. It is not just international or interstate. It is definitely not just interpersonal. Grounded in the picture of Western metaphysics and representative thought, diplomacy is primarily intersubjective. But it is intersubjective in the sense that the diplomatic process takes place between constructed subjects whose very construction relies on the intercourse and mutual recognition of diplomacy. At its basic level, diplomacy is a regulated process of communication between at least two subjects, conducted by their representative agents over a particular object. This, however, should not be treated as an answer to the theoretical quest and question of diplomacy but, rather, as a gathering of persistent question marks: What . . . ? Why . . . ? How . . . ? First, the question of communication arises: what processes does it involve, how is it managed, and how is it akin to ways of manipulation? Second, this understanding raises the question of subjectivity: how does it involve the construction of subjects capable of having relations with each other (the construction of a self and an other of a worth communicating status), and why does it involve these particular subjects and not others? Third, it refers to the question of agency: what is the actual work of diplomacy, and how is representative action personified in the representative (in other words, the accreditation process by which one is charged to speak in the name of the sovereign subject)? Finally, it involves the question of objectification: what are the legitimate areas of intervention and regimes of practice, and how are they determined?

In the end, the conclusion I want to draw is that we need to pay critical attention to the condition of possibility of our diplomacies. For it is the closure of representation that framed—and continuously frames—the ambassadors. The ambassadors are called on to observe and serve the animated picture. They are asked to carry on with their professional work. They are asked to keep faith in what they see and in their diplomatic representations. They are asked to maintain their standing in the sensible picture. They are warned that the slightest unprofessional pose can destroy their trait and, indeed, their portrait. The conventional message: beware of losing a famous and useful picture by messing with its frame, by attending to the limit condition.

But the critical posing of the frame is worth pursuing, I think, if only to revaluate the picture. A closer examination of the diplomatic picture and its animation process can offer, as I have suggested above, a valuable, different, and perhaps wider view of the diplomatic framework, of how diplomatic representation works, and of what the diplomatic service amounts to. One last look, a distant point of view: unless, and until, the ambassadors realize their predicament (and potential), they are destined to remain attuned to the framing and to take their diplomacies for real.

THEORIS

ius legationis

The sending of a diplomatic mission was long considered as the expression of the right of legation (ius legationis) *which again was one of the main attributes of sovereignty.* . . . *The Vienna Convention on Diplomatic Relations, by recognizing that sending and receiving a mission are discretionary acts of States, deprived the* ius legationis *of any real content.*—LUDWIK DEMBINSKI, The Modern Law of Diplomacy

The Embassy of Theory

Theory can be no more than this: a trap set in the hope that reality will be naive enough to fall into it.—JEAN BAUDRILLARD, The Transparency of Evil

I decide to send an embassy. I want to send a message, engage in a dialogue. I name my ambassador, the carrier of my logos. I authorize him to speak in my name. I give him a destination; I destine him. I let him go in a travelog. He reaches the destination. He gets accredited. He gives the message. His logos now represents me.

I, therefore, present a story of diplomacy but also a simple theory of it. One would be justified to argue, however, that I make up a Kissinger-type theory out of a personalized story of diplomacy.[1] Or, that I begin this chapter by setting a trap. Rightly so. But what if I could in fact be taken to be a sovereign of a kind? And what if my word is an ambassador? What if this line is the travelog? What if you, the reader, are the destination, accrediting every word that represents me? Is there a chance of capturing reality in such theory? Could a theory of language be such extraordinary embassy?

It appears extreme but still not inappropriate, I think, to suggest that this diplomatic fable exhibits nothing less than the story of modernity, and especially the culmination of Cartesian reasoning Man as the origin of logos, the sovereign authority behind the word he speaks or writes. The modern condition could therefore concern a sovereign who enjoys the *ius legationis* and has the capacity to send embassies and messages representative of his thought. Yet I go as far as to argue that not just modernity but the whole story of metaphysics amounts to a long history of accrediting the embassy, of tak-

31

ing the message for real—although in metaphysics, unlike modernity, the accrediting sovereign may not be simply the rational being, as the center of logos could shift instead to god or *physis*.

If this initial line of thinking seems to be forcing an embassy over foreign territory (forcing diplomatic reasoning on what is thought to be philosophical ground), it is still nothing undiplomatic. One need look only at how the Western powers forced their permanent legations on the Chinese emperor in the nineteenth century to realize that nonreciprocated representation in foreign realms forms part of the transgressive logic and conventional history of diplomacy.[2] My answer, therefore, to the disciplinarian charge that I am abusing discursive boundaries by not conforming to prearranged terminology or technical language—concerning the mixing of international relations, politics, philosophy, etymology, mythology, literature, and the arts in general—will surely be that I am just being diplomatic! And so, I maintain and am prepared to argue below that one can speak of theoretical embassies, ambassadors, and messages that at the same time create and reveal the real through a classic diplomatic act. Diplomatic theory, in this respect, does not simply focus on technological questions of raison d'état (reason of state) but, rather, primarily on ontological ones of raison d'être (reason of being).

Still, a political review of theory is all the more necessary if the presuppositions and distinctions taken for granted in the discourse of diplomacy are to be rethought. The political question is inseparable from the theoretical one. As Heidegger argues, both are linked ab initio: "The sustaining ground and determining essence of all political Being consists in nothing less than the 'theoretical.'"[3] One cannot understand the political without attempting to understand first the theoretical. But note how the rethinking of theory is itself a political process, for it refers explicitly to the consideration of the politics of enframing that work for the production of diplomatic reality.

Rethinking or politicizing theory is important because of the way theory ties our thinking and politics to a particular understanding of Being:

> The conception of knowledge as "theoretical" is undergirded by a particular interpretation of Being; such a conception has meaning and is correct only on the basis of metaphysics. . . . The "theoretical" is not merely something distinguished and differentiated from the

"practical," but is itself grounded in a particular basic experience of Being.[4]

Theory is, therefore, "a particular interpretation of Being," which since Plato engages in a specific mode of producing knowledge that is attached to technology, representative thought, and metaphysics. As Hubert Dreyfus argues:

> The traditional misunderstanding of human being starts with Plato's fascination with theory. The idea that one could understand the universe in a detached way, by discovering the principles that underlie the profusion of phenomena, was, indeed, the most powerful and exciting idea since fire and language. But Plato and our tradition got off on the wrong track by thinking that one could have a theory of everything—even human beings and their world—and that the way human beings relate to things is to have an implicit theory about them.[5]

Theory exhibits a system of knowledge that is responsible for the closure of Western metaphysics. In Heidegger's terminology, it is a system that engages in the "forgetfulness of Being"—in other words, a forgetting of that which is responsible for whatever is, responsible for beings that are in general.

Note, however, how this historical task of thinking Being could be said to be akin to the act of embassy, for Heidegger charges Being with a special mission:

> In the beginning of Western thinking, Being is thought, but not the "It gives" (es gibt) as such. The latter withdraws in favour of the gift which It gives. That gift is thought and conceptualized from then on exclusively as Being with regard to beings.
> *A giving which gives only its gift, but in the giving holds itself back and withdraws, such a giving we call sending. According to the meaning of giving which is to be thought in this way, Being—that which it gives—is what is sent.* Each of its transformations remains destined in this manner. What is historical in the history of Being is determined by what is sent forth in destining, not by an indeterminately thought up occurrence.[6]

In terms of sending and giving, therefore, theory (which is the highest actualization and technologization of Western thinking) attains the functions of a philosophical embassy. Being is what gives, and Being is what is sent. In the embassy of theory, Being figures as the ambassador par excellence. If the idea of what It represents is to shine, if the thing It gives is to acquire a sovereign standing, Being—just like any ambassador—has to withdraw. If Being does not withdraw, that which It gives can have no autonomous existence or truth.

Similarly, in the case of the embassy, if the work of the embassy does not withdraw, that which is given (the word, the message, the signature) has no representative authority, no truth in itself, for the embassy could represent nothing but itself. The presence of the embassy withdraws in order for the sovereign to appear and be represented. For if it stands there, if one realizes that the embassy is all there is (that is, the sovereign is absent in perpetuity), then there could be no interstate dialogue. That is why in representation the withdrawal of the presence of the embassy effects the advent of the sovereign, allows the sovereign to come through and attain a metaphysical (Heidegger would say, ontic) existence.

But for Heidegger what is withdrawn should not be forgotten. Forgetfulness equals metaphysics. If the work of the embassy is forgotten, diplomacy simply functions and is understood as a practice dealing with relations between sovereigns; just as when Being is forgotten, metaphysics functions and lays claim as a sovereign thinking activity engaged in reflection on real entities. The logos of Being exemplifies, therefore, the logic of the embassy in the historical sending of language as a message sent forth in history, a message that is itself historically determined, being the product of the gathering together (*legein*) of previously received messages (*logoi*). Theory is the technological culmination of negotiating this extraordinary envoy, Being, and its language has a peculiarly diplomatic mode of presencing. Theory is an aboriginal embassy (I expand this point in the next chapter).

Here it is important to note, however, that in Heidegger's "eschatological embassy" not only Being but also the original message has been forgotten, "driven into the extremities of oblivion through a series of gradual erasures and fainter appearances, which by a logic of reversal, occasion a new dispatch."[7] The human condition is neither that of a subject nor of a sovereign, but primarily that of a *Dasein*: a being-there, a diplomatic post. This topographical, spatiotemporal existentialism means that the *Dasein* is responsible for the bearing, sending, and receiving of messages across the epochs and is inevitably committed to the task of their interpretation, committed to respond and to give logos. Giving logos and interpreting is a hermeneutical task. It is both linguistic and political, for hermeneutics is explicitly associated with Hermes, the deity of language and diplomacy: "Hermes is the divine messenger. He brings the message of destiny; *hermeneuein* is that exposition which brings tidings because it can listen to a message."[8] For Heidegger, consequently, hermeneutics does not mean "just interpretation but, even before it, the bearing of message and tidings" (29). Heidegger defines his philosophical project in terms of phenomenological thinking, a form of thinking that does not forget but in fact recollects and looks for the messages that come before, and with, appearances (30). Put differently, it reinterprets the new dispatch not through explanatory models or technical concerns but through the forgotten, original, or primordial messages buried down in the historical archives of the diplomatic post. To that extent, recalling the embassy of Hermes and the hermeneutical go-between, functions for Heidegger as both a mythological and a linguistic reminder of what postmetaphysical thinking should involve.

If, however, the hermeneutical task is simply that of retrieving, receiving, and delivering messages, then the question arises whether Heidegger offers us a highly determined system of thinking, which is still metaphysical, with predetermined messages, missions, and missionaries. Heidegger, nonetheless, is careful to stress that the destiny of Being is in its destination, in "what is sent forth in destining."[9] That is to say, Being has a destination, but this destination cannot be politically determined. Being's destiny can never be a foreclosed question. No one can accredit the ultimate emissary, no one can destine a Hermes. Language speaks itself, and thinking carves its own way: "Questioning builds a way. . . . The way is a way of thinking. All ways of thinking, more or less perceptibly, lead through language in a manner that is extraordinary."[10]

Theoretical knowledge and philosophical practice expressed in diplomatic mode have also been explored by Jacques Derrida. In a typical opening address to a Strasbourg congress of French-speaking philosophical societies, he begins by pointing out to fellow philosophers that "one might say that we represent something or that we are in representation [*nous sommes en représentation*]."[11] An interesting analogy follows:

> I think . . . of the body of philosophy which can itself be considered a corpus of discursive acts or of texts but also as the body or corporation of subjects, of institutions and of philosophical societies. We are mandated, in one way or another, under some form of legitimacy, to represent these societies here. We may be considered more or less explicitly instructed representatives, delegates, ambassadors, emissaries, I prefer to say envoys. (295–96)

In this quotation, Derrida seems to view philosophical discourses as acts of embassy. The practices of philosophy are proposed to be akin to the practices of diplomacy. The philosophical activity refers to "the envoys we are mandated to be, under the aspect and in the highly regulated time of a kind of spectacle, of exhibition, of discursive if not oratorical performance, in the course of ceremonious, coded, ritualized exchanges" (296).

It is not simply as a useful metaphor that Derrida associates philosophy with diplomacy. He specifically takes issue with the Heideggerian thesis concerning the sending of Being, which is "destined," "sent out" from some origin in history. Derrida speaks, therefore, of an *"envoi* of Being" that functions as a delegation of presence, a delegation charged with the metaphysical task of collecting, carrying, and delivering spatiotemporally specific messages (321). He further expands this point in his essay titled *"Envois,"* in which Being is understood as *"en voie,"* literally as a sending "on the way," as the sending of the en-voy, the re-presentative, and so as "a technology which goes from the courier of Greek or Oriental antiquity, along with the messenger who runs from one place to another."[12] If this is only reminiscent of the acts of embassy described above, Derrida refuses to give this process any metaphysical determination, for an *envoi* can be possible only by means of a *renvoi* (of a return and a sending-back, of a reference to itself). The delegation of presence requires, according to Derrida, a language that is sent before it, in order to refer to it (*renvoyer*) and decode it when the message finally arrives (this is the only way the message can have any meaning). Derrida's point is that the Heideggerian message-gift is also a present, a present that is pre-sent. Because language is pre-sent before the message arrives, re-presentation comes before presence. Pre-sent language is the key to the decipherment of the message.

Derrida's pre-sent proposition is combined with the suggestion that the Heideggerian sending of Being constitutes a logocentric and teleological system of communication. The *logoi* (messages) are sent from one post to another (from *telos* to *telos*), in a system that is predetermined to be so, that is, destined from sender (*destinateur*) to addressee (*destinaire*).[13] That Being has an origin and a destination is for Derrida a politically risky assumption. There can be no guarantee as to where the embassy came from, or whether primordial presence finally arrived:

> If the post (technology, position, "metaphysics") is announced at the first *envoi*, then there is no longer A metaphysics, etc. . . . nor even AN *envoi*, but *envois* without destination. For to co-ordinate the different epochs, halts, determinations, in a word the entire history of Being with a destination of Being is perhaps the most outlandish postal lure. There is not even the post or the *envoi*, there are *posts* and *envois*.[14]

The dissemination of meaning, the shifting of interpretive boundaries, the differential interplay of signifiers (iteratable and alterable), that is, the impossibility of effective or ideal communication, precludes the contextual determination of the mission of Being. Whereas Heidegger appears prepared to grant the destiny of Being, indeed the whole history of Being (as "the epochs of the destiny of Being") in the destination of "what is sent forth in destining," for Derrida Being has neither an origin, nor a primordial message, nor a destination, and definitely no destiny we can speak of. As John Caputo explains:

> Derrida undoes the notion of the "meaning" or "truth" of Being, of a primordial epoch which was granted a privileged experience of Being, of a postal service sending "dispatches" (communications) across the epochs, of a primordial sender (*Ereignis*) and a privileged recipient (man), of a special message which, after a period of oblivion, comes safely home again.[15]

There are still *envois,* but they are always outspoken, already voiced (*en voix*) on their way to being (*en voie de l'être*).[16] In terms of an embassy of theory, this would render the *envois* as freelance ambassadors and freelance theorists, with no destination other than the path they travel, with nothing to represent but the language that represents them. Meaning is not something delivered or retrieved at some destination or post, but something recovered from the "traces" of the journey.

So, with Derrida, there is no special need, unlike with Heidegger, to retrieve and decipher some supposed original message as if it had been sent across the epochs. Heidegger's mission of Being seems to presuppose a primordial embassy or a primordial message that is either eschatological or teleological. Derrida, however, by rejecting the credentials of Heidegger's notion of an epochal embassy, postpones the delivery of any ultimate or final message, for he maintains that there is no definitive message as such—and no message at all unless the embassy is accredited. This infinite postponement of the delivery of *the* message is what amounts to the Derridean deferral of meaning—but also, it should be emphasized, a deferral of the end, an end that inevitably comes with the message of the most original embassy, the one sent from the place furthest away (in history), an interpretive end that effectively amounts to the delivery of a final and absolute vocabulary.

Avoiding this situation is very important for Derrida because the delivery of a revelatory truth-dispatch heralds what he calls the moment of Apocalypse: "Truth is the end and the instance of the Last Judgement."[17] Everything will be measured and judged accordingly. All forms of discourse involve, in effect, an apocalyptic risk:

> And if the dispatches [*envois*] always refer to other dispatches without decidable destination, the destination remaining to come, then isn't this completely angelic structure [*angelos* in ancient Greek meant messenger], that of Johannine Apocalypse, isn't it also the structure of every scene of writing in general?. . . . wouldn't the apocalyptic be a transcendental condition of all discourse, of all experience itself, of every mark or every trace? (87)

Derrida insists that we can take neither divine nor mundane *envois* at their word, for they cannot know where their word came from, they cannot determine the origin of language that is the code that precedes and makes intelligible their message:

> We do not know (for it is no longer of the order of knowing) to whom the apocalyptic dispatch [*envoi*] returns; it leaps from one place of emission to the other (and a place is always determined starting from the presumed emission); it goes from one destination, one name, and one tone to the other; it always refers to [*renvoie à*] the name and to the tone of the other that is there but as having been

there before yet coming, no longer being or not yet there in the present of the *récit* [account, history]. (87)

Even the most sovereign, it seems, cannot precede but only come out
of language. As the Holy Scriptures declare: "In the beginning was
the word [*logos*], and the word was with god, and god was the word
[*kai o theos en o logos*]." (John I:1). That is why the embassies that
maintain that they carry the truth of their origin and the origin of
their truth should not be accredited:

> We continue to deny the imposter apostles, the "so-called envoys"
> who are not sent [*envoyés*] by anyone, the false and the unfaithful
> ones, the turgidness and the inflation of those charged with a historic
> mission of whom nobody has requested anything and whom nobody
> has charged or entrusted with anything. Thus shall we continue, in
> the best apocalyptic tradition, to denounce the false apocalypses?[18]

By stripping away the privilege of an embassy of theory to deliver
the message, Derrida desolemnizes philosophy. He challenges the
high status of the theoric embassy—which is the status of metaphysical thought—as narrated by Plato more than two millennia ago (I
deal with Plato's embassy discourse in the next chapter). Derrida's
sacrilege of the philosophical embassy results from his insistence that
not only the positivist but also the Heideggerian circle of the sending
and receiving of messages cannot be closed. Any theory that closes
the circle is logocentric, for it reaches a destinal state of being, a
gathering or sovereign post, a *telos* that accredits presence. Derrida,
therefore, contests both the message and the medium, both the logos
and the method of delivery.

What are we left with? Can we still theorize? Can we still speak
of an embassy of theory and a theory of diplomacy? Yes, because an
embassy of theory that is stateless and carries no sovereign message
offers a different theoretical approach to the study of diplomacy and
may be more at ease with the philosophical circumstances of late
modernity. As Jean Baudrillard explains:

> What good is theory? If the world is hardly compatible with the con-
> cept of the real which we impose upon it, the function of theory is
> certainly not to reconcile it, but on the contrary, to seduce, to wrest
> things from their condition, to force them into an over-existence
> which is incompatible with that of the real. Theory pays dearly for
> this in a prophetic autodestruction. Even if it speaks of surpassing the

economic, theory itself cannot be an economy of discourse. It must become excessive and sacrificial to speak about excess and sacrifice. It must become simulation if it speaks about simulation, and deploy the same strategy as its object. If it speaks about seduction, theory must become seducer, and deploy the same stratagems. If it no longer aspires to a discourse of truth, theory must assume the form of a world from which truth has withdrawn. And thus it becomes its very object.[19]

In the chapters that follow, I adopt the Heideggerian-Derridean approach combined with Baudrillard's theoretical strategy. This entails retrieving originary understandings of theory and diplomacy (Heidegger); exposing the dissemination of *envois* and their logos (Derrida); and recognizing that if theory is to speak about diplomacy, it must itself become diplomatic and employ fully the stratagems and discourses of diplomacy (Baudrillard). In this latter aspect, theory becomes the object of diplomacy and the very object of itself, by constantly reflecting on the terms and categories that it employs, for "it is not enough for theory to describe and analyse, it must itself be an event in the universe it describes."[20] To that extent, such theoretical strategy utilizes the diplomatic discourse employed in interstate relations against states themselves and the static rendition of world politics they normalize and perpetuate. This approach attempts, in short, to challenge the conventional order of things by uncovering the condition that brings it into existence—the logos (the language and the logic) that gathers things, keeps them together, and sustains them in an orderly and hierarchical manner.

THEORIA

fait accompli

The classic tactic for altering the situation unilaterally is by means of a fait accompli—the creation of an accomplished fact. According to this method the opponent is faced with an irreversible change which he cannot revoke whether he wants to or not. With the passage of time, it is hoped, he will be obliged to reconcile himself to the new reality.—RAYMOND COHEN, International Politics: The Rules of the Game

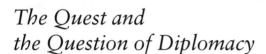

The Quest and
the Question of Diplomacy

The question itself is a path. —MARTIN HEIDEGGER, What Is Philosophy?

I like this improbable confrontation just as others like voyages and diplomacy. There are interpreters everywhere. Each speaking his own language, even if he has some knowledge of the language of the other. The interpreter's ruses have an open field and he does not forget his own interests.
—JACQUES DERRIDA, Limited Inc

The distinction between theory and practice is a philosophical fait accompli. Imagine, however, a crisis between diplomacy and its language: a situation where diplomacy cannot be reconciled to the fait accompli traditionally presented to it in the language of theory and practice; an accustomed practice that cannot be theoretically accounted for. Is this possible?

I will be specific. Take as an example the unique circumstances under which the Holy See engaged in diplomatic relations between 1870 and 1929. During this period, the Holy See continued uninterruptedly to enjoy the right of active and passive legation (to send and receive ambassadors) despite the fact that it neither exercised nor claimed territorial sovereignty.[1] This led to the rise of a double diplomatic corps in Rome, one accredited to the Quirinal and the other to the Holy See, and offered a case unprecedented in the post-Westphalian international system, a system centered on the territorial state, with diplomacy assigned to be the preserve and privilege of it.[2] In short, under the post-Westphalian scheme, nonterritorial

45

units were thought legally and politically incapable of practicing diplomacy.[3]

This issue was taken up in 1878 by Ernest Nys, who voiced the paradox thus:

> From the theoretical point of view there is here a flagrant anomaly. The facts are, however, far from being in conformity with the principles. . . . One of the chief rights of sovereignty, the right of embassy and of negotiation, has been exercised and is still being exercised. *Where is the mistake? Is it on the side of the theory? Or is it on the side of the practice?*[4]

After years of laborious examination searching for the mistake, "the celebrated Brussels authority" published the results: "the mistake" of the diplomatic practice of the Holy See was found to be not diplomatic theory but diplomatic practice itself![5]

This odd conclusion raises a number of questions: how can diplomatic practice ever be at fault? If Nys is right, are we then to say that the ambassadors sent and received by the pope during that period were not actually experiencing and practicing diplomacy— as they thought they were—but something different? Must diplomatic practice always conform to the established principles of diplomatic theory, whatever these are, or vice versa? In the end, how does one search for these principles and how do they lead, if ever, to diplomacy?

I am inclined to take Nys's proposition seriously and not just as an anecdote of deviation after which one can safely return to the certainty of IR concepts and the core facets of the discipline. For Nys rightly pointed out an inconsistency between facts and principles, between action and the systemic scheme that attempts to explain and justify it. He was nonetheless working on this problem within a frame of language that was itself problematic. He reached his critical conclusion by conforming to a well-established fait accompli, one that already understood knowledge in terms of a theory-practice binary opposition, but still one that had difficulties in comprehending an instance of diplomatic practice as diplomatic practice. Nys's response is a rather melodramatic attempt to maintain a high place for theory and secure a fixed concept of diplomacy amidst sovereign practices and contestations that constantly seek to redefine it. By identifying a deviation from normality, and subsequently baptizing a certain event as an anomaly, Nys pointed out the mistake that became the cause—not the effect—of the crisis.

For, if anything, this constitutes a crisis of technical language—a crisis that indicates a breach that can itself be exploited to diverge from the theoretically determined or policy-oriented route of diplomatic investigation. It prompts instead an investigation into the language of diplomacy in terms of a politics of language.[6] That is to say, this crisis provokes the questioning of the tool through which we practice diplomatic theory and put diplomacy to question.

DIPLOMATIC THEORY-PRACTICE

Dangerous distinction between "theoretical" and "practical," e.g., in the case of Kant, but also in the case of the ancients:—they act as if pure spirituality presented them with the problems of knowledge and metaphysics; they act as if practice must be judged by its own measure, whatever the answer of theory may be.—FRIEDRICH NIETZSCHE, The Will to Power

A review of the debates on the diplomatic theory-practice question provides a further justification for politicizing the language of diplomacy, and for the overall necessity of an intervention that takes issue with that language. Note, by way of an introduction, how the theory-practice problematic figures in a classical textbook on IR theory:

> *What is the Relationship between Theory and Practice?* Despite their complementarity, basic differences exist between academic social science theory and political-diplomatic practice. There are also differences, perhaps less basic, between general theoretical approaches to international relations and the "policy sciences" that deal with the foreign policy problems of particular states, just as there are differences between the "policy sciences" and the actual conduct of diplomacy. Each of the several levels of knowledge and action has a legitimacy of its own that ought not to be disparaged by one who happens to be operating at another level. *In all cases it is useful to keep in mind the distinction. . . .*
> Long ago Aristotle differentiated between knowing and doing, between the speculative knowledge and the practical intellect.[7]

Such an approach to the problematic is as interesting as it is rare in IR texts. The authors are aware of and acknowledge the historicity of the theory-practice differentiation, though they seem unwilling to examine the implications of this distinction. Despite the fact that they are writing a book on the *Contending Theories of International Relations*, they are not prepared to seriously contend this issue. They indicate instead that "the interface between theory and practice leads logically to several corollary questions" (17), which are, however, "difficult to answer" (18). The arduousness of such questioning leads to the suspension of further inquiry and justifies the return to the technical concerns of the discipline as addressed by different IR theories.

Such examples of suspending questioning and conforming to the fait accompli of theory-practice are not unimportant. In diplomatic literature, the ontological assumption of this distinction constitutes the starting point for much scholarly discussion. The range of views on the condition of diplomatic theory and its relationship with diplomatic practice is extremely wide. The theory-practice binary opposition appears even to create more theoretical problems than those it seeks to resolve.

Quincy Wright, for example, writes that "diplomats from the time of Kautilya in ancient India and Machiavelli in the Renaissance have written theories of international relations to serve their profession."[8] According to this thesis, theories of diplomacy are well founded in both historical and utilitarian terms. Martin Wight, on the other hand, notes the existence of a normative impossibility in the case of international theory (Wight speaks of "international theory" but discusses it in the context of "diplomacy" and "diplomatic practice"). He suggests primarily that few political thinkers have dealt with diplomacy.[9] In this point he is in agreement with another scholar, Kenneth W. Thompson, who also argues that most of the study of diplomacy has been done by the "diplomatic historian."[10] Wight, however, moves further than that and identifies a tension between theory and practice, for "theory that remains true to diplomatic experience will be at a discount in an age when the belief in progress is prevalent."[11] For Wight, therefore, the impossibility of international theory is the result of progressivism, which is characteristic of modernity. Moreover, "whereas political theory generally is in unison with political activity, international theory (at least in its chief embodiment as international law) sings a kind of descant over against the movement of diplomacy" (29). And in a more poetic tone, Wight adds: "When diplomacy is violent and unscrupulous, international law soars into the regions of natural law; when diplomacy acquires a certain habit of co-operation, international law crawls in the mud of legal positivism" (29). This leads to "a kind of disharmony between international theory and diplomatic practice, a kind of recalcitrance of international politics to be theorized about" (33).

To that extent, for Wight international relations and diplomacy cannot be theorized, cannot be offered a "preferred or desired mode of behaviour" because they are incapable of being improved. Wight seems to understand diplomatic practice within the context of anarchy, which means that any attempt to determine action (that is, to theorize it) is futile. But it is important to note here that for Hedley Bull this anarchic condition hardly presents a problem for the advance of diplomatic theory based on a rationally developed scheme: "Diplomatic theory presents the role of the 'ideal ambassador' in terms of adherence to canons of rationality . . . and the modern diplomatic tradition embodies an attempt to sustain behaviour on this model."[12] Consequently, there seems to be a major gap in the writings of two of the most significant proponents of the English IR school over the possibility of theorizing diplomacy.

If we move to a scholar and practitioner of diplomacy, Harold Nicolson, yet another more detailed view is offered. In contrast to Wight, Nicolson has no doubts over the existence of diplomatic theory, by which he means "a general idea of the principles and methods of international conduct and negotiation."[13] He begins by dismissing the three periods in the development of diplomatic theory as proposed by R. B. Mowat, namely, the disorganized dark ages (476–1475), the organized European States system (1475–1914), and the more modern democratic diplomacy (1918 onward). Instead, Nicolson offers a historical account of the unbroken continuity of diplomatic theory from the ancient Greek city-states, through Roman public law and Canon law, to Byzantine institutions carried over to the diplomatic theory of the Italian city-states. By the mid-sixteenth century when diplomatic theory "begins to assume a modern tinge" (22), two main types can be identified: the warrior or heroic theory and the mercantile or shopkeeper theory. The first has its roots in feudal military castes and approaches diplomacy as "war by other means." The second originates from the contacts of commerce and sees diplomacy as "peaceful negotiation." Nicolson suggests that "each of these two theories has its peculiar dangers as its peculiar illusions" and that both display "idealism and realism" (26, 27). He subsequently groups the two theories into a new binary opposition that is neither developed nor explained: "What really separates them is that the former is essentially a dynamic theory whereas the latter is static. The one needs movement for its expression, the other requires calm" (27). In the end, the reader is left with a cryptic diplomatic formula without any empirical or historical insight of how these "essential" characteristics are expressed in practice.

Another interesting point concerns Nicolson's identification of diplomatic theory as having "a distinct upward curve of progress" that allows him to undertake a holistic approach to the study of diplomacy while recognizing certain discontinuities (17). He states the case as follows: "Yet if we consider the continuity of diplomatic theory and examine the graph of its development, we shall find that this graph (although at every stage of the world's history there have been moments, as now, when it becomes seismographic) does show an ascending line" (23). Nicolson, therefore, also associates diplomatic theory with progressivism (by referring to "continuity," "development," and "an ascending line"); in other words, he tells the story of diplomatic theory through the narrative of progress and modernization that Wight uses to suggest the impossibility of diplomatic theory. Of course, at the other extreme to both Nicolson and Wight, let us not forget Ernest Nys who could rationally argue not only the primacy of diplomatic theory (nonprogressive and absolute) but also the impossibility of certain manifest diplomatic practices, that is, concluding theoretically that an instance of diplomatic practice was not diplomacy.

The most recent work on diplomatic theory comes from James Der Derian. Echoing Wight, he argues:

> Diplomacy has been particularly resistant to theory. . . . Theories of diplomacy, when they do exist, usually consist of underdeveloped and implicit propositions. . . . Neither is there to be found a substantial theoretical work on the subject in the contemporary literature of international relations.[14]

Although Der Derian's diplomatic theory is not without its problems (such as his attempt to develop a poststructuralist approach out of the modernist scheme of Bull and Wight),[15] it provides a good starting point for rethinking the contemporary condition of international-diplomatic theory. In his *Antidiplomacy*, Der Derian states the critical task: "International theory continually confronts institutional pressures to conform, to reduce itself to the reigning dogma, to discipline insurgent antitheses. To keep . . . theory from falling victim to similar perils, one must on occasion take on the role of *agent provocateur*."[16] An apolitical approach to the language of diplomatic theory is to that extent an accessory to the policing and disciplinary practices of the field. Conformity to IR binary oppositions simply results in reproducing an undesirable and highly problematic vocabulary. In this instance, it affects the naturalization of the fait accompli (that is, that elements of theory cannot be found in the territory of practice; one is doing one or the other) and the normalization of grand narratives that pursue, with equal certainty, conflicting formulas and propositions on diplomatic theory and practice.

THE ETYMOLOGICAL QUEST

The word becomes a name for something indeterminate.—MARTIN HEIDEGGER, An Introduction to Metaphysics

By now it is apparent that we are not only dealing with key terms in IR but also with words understood and applied differently. The etymological aspect of theory now intrudes to such a degree that I can no longer hold back the key term: *theoria*. In this section and the next one, I examine the career of the word *theoria* and its etymological-philosophical association with both theory and diplomacy. This approach involves a careful and patient investigation of the vicissitude of the word in order to recover originary meanings of it and so to regain its unimpaired strength. As Heidegger says: "Words and language are not wrappings in which things are packed for the commerce of those who write and speak. It is in words and language that things first come into being and are."[17] Through this lexical intervention, I also attempt to expose the rhetorical delimitations involved in the process of accomplishing the fait accompli of theory/practice and of diplomatic theory/practice. Let us begin by reading some entries from the modern bible of words, *The Oxford English Dictionary*.[18] Sit comfortably, relax, and let our most pertinently diplomatic signifiers present their credentials:

> **theor** *Gr. Antiq.* Also in L. form *the′orus* [mod. ad. Gr. *theor-os* spectator, one who travels in order to see things, also an envoy, ambas-

sador: see THEORY.²] An ambassador or envoy sent on behalf of a state, esp. to consult an oracle or perform a religious rite (Cf. THEORY²).

theoria rare. [a. Gr. *theoria* a looking at, contemplation, f. *theorein* to look at.]
1. ? Contemplation, survey. *Obs. rare.*
2. The perception of beauty regarded as a moral faculty.

theoric, a² Gr. *Antiq.* [ad. Gr. *Theoricos* pertaining to spectacles, f. *theoria* viewing, beholding.] Pertaining to or connected with public spectacles, religious functions, and solemn embassies: applied esp. to a fund provided for these purposes from the public treasury at Athens (Cf. THEORY²).

theoricon Gr. *Antiq.* Also -kon. [a. Gr. *theoricon,* neut. of *theoricos* THEORIC a².] The theoric fund in ancient Athens: see THEORIC a.²

theory¹ Also -ie, -ee. [ad. late L. *theōria* (Jerome in Ezech. XII. xl. 4), a. Gr. *theoria* a looking at, viewing, contemplation, speculation, theory, also a sight, a spectacle, abstr. sb. f. *theoros* (: *-theaoros*) spectator, looker on, f. stem *thea-* of *theasthai* to look on, view, contemplate. In mod. use prob. from med. L. trans. of Aristotle. Cf. It. *teoria* (Florio 1598 *theoría*), F. *théorie* (15. in Godef. *Compl.*).]
1. A sight, a spectacle. *Obs. rare.*
2. Mental view, contemplation. *Obs.*
3. A conception or mental scheme of something to be done, or of the method of doing it; a systematic statement of rules or principles to be followed.
. . . . \5. In the abstract (without article): Systematic conception or statement of the principles of something; abstract knowledge, or the formulation of it: often used as implying more or less unsupported hypothesis (cf. 6): distinguished or opposed to *practice* (cf. 4b). *In theory* (formerly *in the theory*): according to theory, theoretically (opp. to *in practice* or *in fact*)

theory² Gr. *Antiq.* [ad. Gr. *theoria,* the same word as in THEORY¹, in a specialized sense.] A body of THEORS sent by a state to perform some religious rite or duty; a solemn legation.

One crucial observation stems almost immediately from the reading of these quotations: the evolution of the word *theory* out of the ancient Greek word *theoria,* and the import of its link to such words as *theor, theoric,* and *theoricon.*[19] This word *theoria* was used in an-

cient Greek to designate, among other things, an old type of embassy, the solemn or sacred embassy sent to attend religious festivals
and games, discharge the divine obligations of the polis, and consult
the oracle. This particular ancient meaning has been lost in the modern, Anglicized use of the term *theoria,* as is the case with the modern Greek term. The idea of the solemn embassy is currently conveyed in the second entry for *theory,* interestingly named *theory²*.
Through this slight grammatological effacement, meaning is now
locked within a new word, which has its own associations to *theory¹,
practice, theoria,* and so on. Still it is this word theory that I must
now use in English if I want to convey the meaning of the solemn
embassy.

It seems, consequently, that the term/word *theoria* allows us to
cross the disciplinarian boundaries into lexical territories thought
lost and forgotten. Theoria revives etymological, philosophical, and
historical claims over those territories (ancient Greek, Latin, rare,
and obsolete) annexed by static representations of diplomacy and
theory though not quite fully appropriated. The value of theoria lies
not only in its etymological link with theory and the forgotten meaning of the sacred embassy it provides, but also in its relation with
other concepts that are now made possible and relevant by this association. Theoria constitutes my link to theory and by that also to the
quest and question of diplomacy. In this respect, theoria—itself an
embassy—problematizes the theory-practice distinction. It puts forward the view of theory-as-practice.[20]

A closer reading of the etymology of *theoria* reveals the following. Firstly, *theoria* is derived from the words *theos* (god) and *orao*
(to see). It had the meaning "to see god" and particularly referred to
this aspect of eyeing god in the shrine. *Orao* also relates, however, to
the word *hora* (time, hour), and so theoria can be understood as the
moment of god or the moment devoted to god. The sight and time of
theoria invoked therefore a specific truth-making process. As Heidegger explains:

> *Thea* is goddess. It is a goddess that *aletheia,* the unconcealment from
> out of which and in which that which presences, appears to the early
> thinker Parmenides . . . *theoria* is pure relationship to the outward ap-
> pearances belonging to whatever presences, to those appearances
> that, in their radiance, concern man in that they bring the presence of
> the gods to shine forth.[21]

Later, in the biblical tradition, *theoria* was given a special theological significance, for it was specifically used to describe the view of Jesus at the cross, that is, bearing witness to the moment of sacrifice (*epi ten theorian tauten, theorountes ta genomena*).[22]

But the root word *theo* in ancient Greek also meant—depending on the emphasis—to run (*théo*) and to look (*theó*). As run, *theo* is of much older use and can be traced as far back as Homer, who used it in the context of competitive running for a game, of chasing or running after somebody or something, of running away to save one's life.[23] From this root *theo-* (run), *theoria* acquired the meaning of a journey, of traveling abroad to see the world. This meaning is especially important, for it refers to the first known use of the word *theoria* by Herodotus. It was employed to designate the journey of Solon, the lawgiver of Athens, to Egypt and other "far away" places.[24] The importance of the timing of Solon's journey points to the significance of *hora*, the reaching of a certain moment in one's private or political lifetime for going on a theoria. A further derivative meaning of *theoria* is that of the path as *theoris* and as *theorike odos*.[25]

Theo, meaning look, was often used instead of *theaou* or *theomai*, and when combined with *orao* in *theoria* a double emphasis of vision was given to the word. Thus with this second sense of the root *theo-* in mind, *theoria* acquired the meaning of looking at something attentively, of viewing something for a long time, and as a noun it also had the meaning of spectacle and sight in general. In particular, it came to mean what was seen at the *theatron* (theater), the *theatron* itself being the place where theoria was practiced.[26] *Theoria* had, therefore, a number of derivatives and associations with theater: *theama* as spectacle in general and at the *theatron* in particular; *theoros/theoretes*, the spectator (at the theater); *theorion*, the place reserved for seeing and so where the spectators were seated in the theater; *theoreterion*, the very personal place for seeing, the seat of the spectator; *theorikon*, the public fund that paid for the poor citizen's attendance at the theater. Finally, in the sense of hidden view that is revealed to sight, we had the use of the word *theoretra*, which referred to the revelation of statues or the presents given by the groom to the bride when she first unveiled herself.[27]

As used by philosophers and as I extensively show below, *theoria* also meant the sight of truth and had the sense of contemplation and philosophical reasoning. *Theoreton*, for example, meant both what could be seen or watched,[28] and what could be reached by contemplation,[29] or by reason,[30] or by logos.[31] Moreover, *theoreteon* came in a much stronger sense, as that which must be contemplated.[32]

From the integration of all these senses of *theoria*—as journey, as attentive view, and as the sight/moment of god—one can begin to understand the ancient Greek use of *theoria* as sacred embassy. Theoria was sent as the most solemn of embassies and included on the one hand the journey to the shrine, the oracle, or the public games, and on the other the view, the sight of the sacred, or the spectacle of the games. Theorias were sent by the Greek city-states to important shrines to commemorate a religious event, dispatch a religious service, and/or consult the oracle such as in Delphi, Delos, and Nemeau. Theorias were also charged to attend festivities like the Dionysian and Orphic ones, and the four Panhellenic games that included the Olympias. The sacred ambassadors were called theors or *theoroi* and were specially chosen. Demosthenes describes with much honor an event where he was charged as head of a theoria (*architheoros*), "sent in the name of Athens to the Nemeau shrine of Zeus," and where he inaugurated the sacrifice.[33] And Alcibiades boasted the magnificence of his display in the theoria to Olympia where he "entered seven chariots."[34] Theoria was an embassy of paramount importance, and failure to dispatch one could result in divine punishment: "To the people of Athens, the prophet of Zeus announces. Whereas you have let pass the seasons of sacrifice and of the sacred embassy [*theoria*], he bids you to send nine chosen envoys, and that right soon."[35] That theoria was the most solemn of embassies was also shown by the fact that the sacred ambassadors were always crowned and magnificently dressed (the festal robes were known as the *theorika*). Such was its importance that the host city or the relevant shrine assigned special officials (*theorodokoi*) for the reception and treatment of these theors.[36] Finally, the consultation of the oracle, on the value of a policy or the rightness of a planned action, provided the necessary mental unveiling for access to truth, the prophecy, or the *theorema*, and so by following the will of god the right—not the wrong—action was taken.[37]

Theoria then was an embassy to god or truth (tied to divine sanction and authority), and theors were ambassadors, peripatetic "theorists," charged with the discovery of what was right or true. In theoria, therefore, one can view embassy as theory and theory as embassy.

Beyond the etymological association there is a philosophical proposition at issue here: namely, that theory at its Platonic conception was the mirror image of the very diplomatic process it now seeks to explain.

THE VOYAGE OF THEORY

Beware of Greeks bearing gifts.—Roman proverb

To examine the historicity of the contemporary understanding of theory as thinking technique is to start with Plato's interpretation of theoria as the thinking act akin to philosophical contemplation. Plato, however, used *theoria* to convey a number of other meanings, too.[38] In *Phaedo,* Plato employed *theoria* to describe the solemn embassy sent to the Delian oracle "in honour of the god" Apollo and to commemorate Theseus's journey to Crete.[39] In *The Republic,* there are instances where Plato's *theoria* can be understood more generally as participation in any kind of festival or campaign.[40] In *Crito,* theoria is used as journey,[41] and in the *Laws,* in addition to voyage, as view and careful observation.[42] In another instance, it has a more specific meaning when it refers exclusively to the Dionysian celebrations.[43] Finally, Plato employs the word *theoria* to denote the contemplation of the divine,[44] and in his most common usage as speculation and philosophical reasoning.[45]

The diverse uses of *theoria* in Plato can be further illustrated in the first Latin translations of the Platonic works where *theoria* is translated as *spectatio, contemplatio, legatio, pompa solemnis,* and *sacra procuranda,* depending on how the translator reads the context.[46] This is also the case with English versions where the translation of *theoria* is based on a contemporary understanding of what Plato must have meant in the context he was speaking. But why is it then that Plato, aware of all these different senses, still decides to use *theoria* to denote the act of philosophical thinking? Why this particular word?

As already suggested, the word *theoria* indicates sight (*thean*), a term that enjoys a distinctive position in the history of Western philosophy. Among the first places where this economy of gaze is encountered is in book VII of *The Republic,* which contains the famous parable of the cave. In this parable Plato pictures human beings as prisoners in a sort of subterranean cavern, condemned to see only the shadows of beings projected up by the light of a fire outside—not the real beings themselves (*ta onta*). In order to see reality, one must be freed and ascend out of the cave toward the light: "The ascent and the view [*thean*] of the things above is the mind's upward progression into the intelligible region" (517B). Plato employs *thean*, therefore, to describe the mental experience of the real or being (*to on*). Reality (*ontologia*) is equated to the "idea" that is accessible to the gaze of the philosopher (*idon*, *idein* is the past tense of *orao*, to see; the term *idea*, therefore, essentially means what-has-been-seen outside the cave). Furthermore, reality is equated with truth (*aletheia*), what could be seen as standing there (*orthon*) in its unconcealment (*a-lethes*). Reality concerns, therefore, the unveiling of what was previously concealed, the revelation of light (*phos*) as opposed to darkness (517B and D, 518A-D). For Plato, the most significant organ whereby the human being apprehends is the eye (518C). The eye is turned around like the scene-shifting *periact* (triangular prisms) in the theater, until the mind "endures" the sight of the real, that brightest region of being (518C). The idea, what-has-been-seen, forms to that extent the basis for the acquisition of knowledge and virtue. In short, Plato offers an awareness of reality based on visual experience, a particular mode of presence established in the gaze of beings. Theoria, with all its characteristics of viewing and attentive looking, manifestly assumes the central role in this philosophical act.

Journeying, however, is also fundamental to Platonic theoria. For in order to see reality, the philosopher is required to ascend out of the cave. Plato thus describes the return of the philosopher to the cave as a return from a theoria (*theorion epi ta anthropina elthon;* 517D). The return of the philosopher signifies the conclusion of a contemplative journey, a journey that equips the philosopher with theoretical knowledge subsequently communicated for the benefit and education of the people. Theoria constitutes, therefore, the philosophical journey out of the cave of ignorance.

But it is important to note that this is not a journey of any kind. It is not simply a theoria, as understood by Herodotus and denoting a going abroad to see the world. It is a theoria meant for divine contemplations (*theion theorion;* 517D). Just like the sacred embassy, it is sent to contemplate the metaphysical. Compared with mere practical knowledge produced in the cave, the knowledge produced from philosophical thought is, for Plato, of a more divine quality (*theoterou tinos tichanei;* 518E). Later, following Plato, Aristotle would go even further, claiming that the intellect is itself something divine (*theion ho nous*) and that theoretical life is equivalent to divine life (*bios theios*).[47]

Platonic philosophical thinking, therefore, appears to resemble ancient Greek diplomatic practice. By specifically referring to the theoria sent out of the cave as a sacred theoria (*theia theoria*), Plato explicitly ties the act of philosophical thought to the solemn practices of the sacred embassy. On the one hand, Platonic theoria links the privileged position of the philosopher outside the cave (being the one uniquely accessing the truth of beings) to the high status of the few chosen ones charged to be sacred ambassadors. On the other hand, the truth of Platonic theoria—the status of the philosophical logos following the contemplative journey—is rhetorically tied to the divine logos of the gods transmitted through the oracle.

Elsewhere Plato is even more explicit in his appropriation of diplomatic practices. He presents in the *Laws* a system for his perfect republic, a republic in which ambassadors and theors are implicated in pedagogy. Here he particularly speaks of their role in the education of youth concerning the laws and affairs of the polis (951A). This was a role traditionally reserved for the man of philosophy, but Plato appears also to expect pedagogical responsibility from the man of diplomacy.

A detailed discussion is found in the section of the *Laws* dealing with the questions of going abroad and of the admission of foreigners (950D–953E). In this section, the pedagogical proposition for theoria is also put forward; significantly, this time *theoria* is specifically used to denote a solemn embassy and/or a journey abroad. Plato begins by establishing certain conditions under which a citizen could travel abroad. First, nobody under the age of forty would be permitted to do so under any circumstances (*midami midamos*). Second, nobody would be permitted to go abroad in a private capacity—only in a public one, which involves only the sending of heralds (*kerixin*), embassies (*presbeiais*), and theorias (*theorois*) (military expeditions as a special category were excepted; 950D, E). So the journey out of the Platonic polis is restricted to old people (note that the word for an old person and for an ambassador was the same, *presbes*) and specifically to those engaging in diplomatic activities (heralds, ambassadors, theors). But of all the diplomatic functions, special importance is again given to theoria. That is why the theor is required to be over fifty years of age (and under sixty), of high repute in political and military affairs, and always dispatched with the approval of the law-wardens. Plato emphasizes the importance of sending solemn embassies to the Pythian Apollo, the Olympian Zeus, Nemeau, and the Isthmus, and the participation in the sacrifices and the games in honor of the gods. But, in addition, a significant function of theoria lies in the survey of new and unknown things, the inspection of the doings of other peoples (*ta ton allon anthropon pragmata theoresai;* 951A). Furthermore, such theoria is exclusively intended to communicate with "those few people who are divinely inspired" (*anthropoi aei theioi tines, ou polloi*). In the search for such people, no journey (*theoria*) must be spared either by land or by sea (951B).

The information and knowledge acquired by such theorias is then to be communicated to the citizens of the model polis to confirm the rightness of its laws or to amend the deficient ones. Theoria is of absolute importance, "for without it, or in misconducting it, the polis will not remain perfect" (*aneu gar autes tis theorias kai zetiseos ou menei pote teleos polis, oud'an kakos autin theorosin;* 951C). Theoria is therefore charged with the discovery of the good and held responsible for the perfect condition of the polis. Of course, that was precisely the role saved for the philosopher-ruler in *The Republic*.[48]

In the *Laws*, consequently, the Platonic republic attains its full metaphysical significance. It becomes a political cave. Only certain persons are allowed or can endure the journey out of it. Note that both philosophers and solemn envoys engage in theoria: the former travel a contemplative journey while the latter travel a political one. Both are united in a theoretical travelog. Theoria is a means to another world, concerned with the beyond; the diplomatic theoria is concerned with what is beyond the walls of the polis, and the contemplative one, with what is beyond the limits of the philosophical cave. It is typical of Platonic irony that Socrates, the nontraveling philosopher becomes a model of the theoretician. Socrates is a philosopher who contemplates *aporia* and yet he himself is an *aporos* (without passage or way), one who has never crossed to the beyond (*peras*). Socrates never left the city for a journey, never joined a sacred embassy; in fact, Plato says that he only once crossed the walls of the polis. This man, Socrates, who has never been on a theoria (who is different precisely by not being on a theoria of any kind), is charged with the highest theoretical mission, to undertake the most difficult journey of all.

In this respect, we should read *The Republic* as a parody of the limited capabilities of theoria but also focus on how these fascinating aspects of theoric journey finally get lost, particularly in the process of developing a systematic theoretical scheme. For in identifying the philosopher's theory with his ideas (*idein* as what-has-been-seen), Plato demotes and marginalizes the journey out of the cave. Once the light is encountered, once the truth is revealed, once reality is viewed, the quest is passé and the path that led there loses its significance. Similarly, the journey that made contemplation possible in the first place falls into oblivion. So in associating being with what-has-been-seen, the Platonic idea becomes an idol (*eidolon*) in the mirror of which theoria is now immediately discharged.

The distinction between theory and practice gets formally established by Aristotle. Plato offered a scheme, "more complex and far less articulate," when the contemplative life of the philosopher was contrasted with the life of other men who pursued the "love of the body" (*philosomatos*), "the love of honor" (*philotimos*), and "the love of riches" (*philochrematos*).[49] As it happens, Hans Morgenthau locates the theory-practice distinction in Plato's *Theaetetus*, the differentiation "between what is worth knowing intellectually and what is useful for practice."[50] Still, Aristotle seems to provide a clearer distinction of the three prominent lives men could live[51]: either (a) a "life of enjoyment" (*bios apolaustikos*), (b) a "life of politics" (*bios politikos*), or (c) a "life of contemplation" (*bios theoritikos*).[52] Aristotle defines the political life as a "life of practice" (*bios praktikos*), and by that he refers to a life of active participation in the affairs of the polis. He even goes as far as to argue that the end of politics is not knowledge (*gnosis*) but practice (*praxis*).[53] Moreover, in his *Politics* Aristotle describes the theoretical life of the philosopher as a life in exile, an alien life (*bios xenikos*), and as a life detached from the political community (*politikes koinonias apolelimenos*).[54] To that extent, Aristotle first equates political life exclusively with practice and then excludes from politics the life of the philosopher. The philosopher's theoretical life is nonetheless praised as engaging in an activity (*energeia*) of the highest virtue.[55]

The demise of the political-diplomatic aspect of theoria follows its obliteration of the journey and the establishment of the theory-practice binary opposition. Consequently, philosophical thought as theoric embassy was a short-lived notion: at least from the historical evidence we have, it began and ended with Plato. Aristotle dediplomatized theory in two ways. First, as argued above, he depoliticized theory by contrasting theoretical life with political life (*bios theoretikos* and *bios praktikos/politikos*). Second, he substituted the theoric journey out of the cave and leading to the idea with bare, non-political (of no direct relevance to the affairs of the polis) work or action (*energeia*). In this, Aristotle proposes an ahistorical movement from what is (*ti estin*) to that which is and is out of the mind (*oti estin, exo tes dianoias*). The theoretical act could be arduous, for the theoria of truth (*he peri tes aletheias theoria*) can be difficult because of limitations of reason, but still theoria is not elitist and solemn as in the Platonic sense; so it is possible in the combination of different attempts to reason.[56] Theoria becomes an *episteme* whose end is the investigation of first principles and causes.[57] In Aristotle, therefore, not only is theoria depoliticized, but it also loosens its links with ontology and starts to concern itself with epistemology. This epistemologizing of theoria was later to be endorsed by Aristotle's students at the Academy, where only the contemplative walk (*peripatos*) remained as a ritual reminder perhaps of the theoric journey of philosophy.[58]

So whereas theory and practice were not viewed in opposing terms for those philosophers who preceded Aristotle, by the time of the Neoplatonists the distinction was fully established and normalized. For some the distinction came to mean that practical life was linked to *apolaustic* life (a life of action and enjoyment) and theoretical life as life of truth and personal perfection.[59] Later, the Christian doctrine reinforced the distinction between *vita activa* and *vita contemplativa* (following the biblical example of Martha and Maria in Luke 10:41–42), that is, between the essential requirements of Christian life, active charity, compassion, and acts concerned with the welfare of others (*erga anankaia*) and those of divine contemplation, detachment, and abstinence that were deemed more demanding.[60] Later, in Augustine, the theory-practice distinction figures in terms of *scientia*, the right use of worldly things, and *sapientia*, the contemplation of divine things.[61]

In the modern period, according to Nicholas Lobkowicz, Descartes reconsidered the distinction of the theoretical and the practical only to reestablish a new distinction reminiscent of it—that is, between mathematical, scientific reasoning on the one hand and action as "bare will" on the other (117–20). Immanuel Kant maintained the distinction by viewing theory as "what belongs to the being of a thing" and practice as "what should belong to it *per libertatem*, in terms of freedom," and reached extreme conclusions such as the argument that "ethics holds true in theory and not in practice" (120–22). In Georg W. F. Hegel, the differentiation seems to attain its full metaphysical significance: "The distinction between thought and will is only that between the theoretical attitude and the practical" (quoted in Lobkowicz, 150–52). But both are united in the spirit (*geist*): Spirit is thought, and spirit is also will. Following Hegel, Karl Marx attempts (through the revolutionary spirit, which he renames praxis) to integrate the theoretical revolution, the new order of thought, and the practical revolution, the new order of being (274–76). But in suggesting the overcoming of false consciousness through revolutionary praxis, which would lead in the harmonic coexistence between theory and practice, Marx also makes the presupposition of a primary tension between the two in the state of social alienation.

Thus the separation and contrast of theory and practice figure in Aristotle (that is, not opposed in Plato and not at all apparent in the pre-Socratic thinkers). Subsequently, the distinction gets historically established and becomes normalized in the early Christian and Renaissance thinkers. It is, therefore, not an absolute or natural opposition but one that is historically and discursively produced.

THE TRACE OF DIPLOMACY

In view of the thesis outlined above, the notion of theoria challenges the conventional understanding of theory and diplomacy. Theoria blurs both the diplomacy-theory distinction and the theory-practice one. As shown, these separations are foundational for the IR discipline and their methodological ramifications a source of considerable dispute. Concerns about the gap between theory and practice, or the discovery of the best theory to describe diplomatic practice, become secondary when examined in the light of the genealogical implications of theoria. For the act of theory is already presupposed in the discourse of practice, and even more so in diplomatic practice. The act of solemn embassy (the journey, the rite, the transmitted prophecy) fundamentally concerns, and cannot be separated from, the act of theoretical contemplation (eyeing the divine, disclosing the truth of beings). Theoria reminds us that it is not possible to send an embassy in practice alone. For the embassy must be sighted, contemplated in advance, and so "theorized" as the very embassy that it is. Similarly, theory is not beyond action, and as argued in the *ius legationis* section, not beyond diplomatic action; its association with Western metaphysical thought suggests that it functions through acts of sovereign representation as is the case with diplomacy. To utilize the term *theoria* is, therefore, to elide the problems established through the language of (diplomatic) theory and practice, unsettle their status as real problems, and substitute the constitutive role of language as the core problematic.

To reject the fait accompli that separates theory from practice is to begin walking on the path of theoria, to read embassy as theory and theory as embassy. The way this act is represented remains nonetheless important. To propose theoria as a new methodology for understanding diplomacy is to accredit a new sovereign center in the shadow of which the truth of other representations will have to be measured and decided. That is why to embark on a theoria should not involve specific theoretical missions or ways—at least not as a precondition for practicing it. It should not be just a venture into the known, not merely a re-search, if by this term we mean a repetition of theoretical inquiries or empirical verification of hypotheses. It should also be, I think, an adventure, a quest, and a query into the unthought, with a willingness to deviate from the way (the safety of the single way or the comfort of the mainstream, *meth'-odos*). More important, it ought to attempt to open up ways of thinking that surpass technical theorizing. In other words, to understand theoria not as a contemplative moment but as a historical—and ultimately political—journey is to reverse the Platonic and post-Platonic position that turned theoria into a technical interpretation of thinking, "a process of reflection in service to doing and making."[62] To approach theoria as primarily a journey is to free it from the mode of calculative thinking, which though responsible for scientific enlightenment is also the beginning of metaphysics.[63] In this respect, moving from theory to theoria is finally a way of restating language—and not national interest or interstate management—as the primary question of diplomacy.

THEMA

coup de main

A sudden vigorous attack [F. lit., stroke of the hand].—The
Oxford English Dictionary

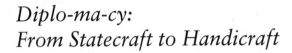

Diplo-ma-cy:
From Statecraft to Handicraft

Meanwhile, however—and concurrently with this evolution from the herald to the orator and the orator to the professional diplomatist—a further factor had gradually emerged. This factor was concerned in a curious way with the origin of the word "diplomacy" itself.—HAROLD NICOLSON, Diplomacy

Perhaps thinking, too, is just something like building a cabinet. At any rate, it is a craft, a "handicraft." "Craft" literally means the strength and skill in our hands. . . . Only a being who can speak, that is, think, can have hands and can be handy in achieving works of handicraft.—MARTIN HEIDEGGER, What Is Called Thinking?

Terence Bishop's *Scriptores Regis* begins by suggesting that "the charters of Henry I, Stephen, and Henry II may be exposed to advanced criticism by identifying, in originals, the several hands of royal scribes."[1] In this same text there is an interesting definition of diplomatic theory as the "study of official handwriting" (3). For the student of international relations used to understanding the concept of diplomacy in terms of statecraft and the word *diplomacy* as part of an exclusive political vocabulary, this may come as a surprise. Such "diplomatic" understandings constitute unwelcome lexical complications, for the science of interstate diplomatic contacts is thought to be something separate from the science of diplomatics and paleography.

Still, I think this aberration merits our attention. It provides an opportunity to examine language not as an unproblematic medium of communication but as a depository of contested interpretations. Furthermore, as I suggest below through an etymological and genea-

69

logical study of diplomacy, the work of the hand and the theme of handicraft, far from being linguistic exceptions or anomalies, actually figure as prominent factors in the textual construction of what goes by the name *diplomacy*. I do not refer here simply to the way the hand is employed in contemporary diplomatic contacts to convey different messages, as in the case of handshake techniques, warm embraces, or triumphant salutes.[2] Nor do I speak of handicraft in the sense of calligraphy, the "high qualifying standard in . . . handwriting," required in the nineteenth-century examinations for entrance to the British Diplomatic Service,[3] and something that became a personal obsession to Lord Palmerston when receiving dispatches from diplomats abroad.[4] These instances offer a highly determined interpretation of handicraft in the service of official correspondence and statecraft, whereas, for the purposes of this chapter, the hand's significance is in the way it indicates diplomatic themes forgotten or neglected in the policy-oriented rendition of diplomacy. The crafts of the hand attempt to interpret diplomacy differently, suggesting that the crafts of the state were not and so should not be the only way one explains or speaks about diplomacy.

Two interlinked propositions are made in the process. The first suggests that thinking about diplomacy cannot be separated from speaking or writing diplomacy. I take it, to that extent, that the thing-word, signified-signifier binary opposition does not hold, and so our attempts to delineate the theme of diplomacy cannot be examined in isolation to our attempts to craft a word to name it and to mean it. The second proposition concerns the process of thematizing diplomacy—what its practice involves and what understandings its name (and its thematic roots) introduce—and how this theoretical process can be understood to be itself a diplomatic one. In other words, it maintains the main thesis of this book that theorizing diplomacy is another way of practicing it. By following the crafts of the hand that themselves carry a theme of diplomacy, this chapter rethinks the path of theoria as a thematic condition that is not disassociated from diplomatic practice.

The *coup de main* begins by examining how attempts to delineate absolute themes of diplomacy fail to foreclose the thematic question. Then the role of the hand is considered in helping us to rethink diplomacy, that is, philosophically to open up diplomatic themes to critical investigation. Then the history of the word *diplomacy* and its association with diplomas, royal inscriptions, and official handwriting are examined in some detail. Finally, the role of the double hand in signing authorial sovereignty through duplicitous writing and as a theme of diplomacy is investigated.

THEMES OF DIPLOMACY

The purpose of this monograph is to describe, in simple but precise forms, what diplomacy is and what it is not.—HAROLD NICOLSON, Diplomacy

"Diplomacy" is, after all, a notoriously flexible word. Our American cousins have long used it, sometimes, as a synonym of foreign policy. There might once have been some sniping at the lack of rigour which this can be seen to imply.—ALAN JAMES, *"Diplomacy,"* Review of International Studies

There have been numerous endeavors to define the theme and subject matter of diplomacy in contemporary IR theory. A particularly long and detailed venture is offered in the book of a retired Portuguese ambassador, José Calvet De Magalhães, titled *The Pure Concept of Diplomacy*. The book makes the case that conceptual purification is both possible and necessary. The following quotation is a summary of the results:

The concept of diplomacy, according to us, can be defined as follows:

a) an instrument of foreign policy
b) for the establishment and development of peaceful contact between the governments of different states
c) through the use of intermediaries
d) mutually recognized by the respective parties.

These intermediaries are called *diplomatic agents*.

Diplomacy thus understood is called by us *pure diplomacy* to distinguish it from all other senses in which the word diplomacy is frequently used, some of which include elements that have nothing to do with diplomatic activity, while others lack one or more of the essential elements of the definition given above. A pure theory of diplomacy that allows us to understand this old institution in its exact form and perspective can be built only on the foundation of a precise concept of this kind. In the state of conceptual confusion in which the theory and history of foreign policy find themselves, the formulation of such a pure theory seems to us to be required in order to clarify ideas and avoid mistaken notions that have generated a number of practical negative consequences. . . . The goal of the present study is precisely to try to isolate conceptually, through the application of a pure concept of diplomacy, what belongs to diplomacy as a pure instrument of foreign policy, eliminating from its study the elements that do not belong to it and serve only to confuse concepts. It may be a doomed enterprise if we think that not much progress has been made in separating the two in political literature, since Harold Nicolson vehemently protested against the confusion between diplomacy and foreign policy in 1939, in the first edition of his essay *Diplomacy*. The confusion is rife especially in American academic literature, which is certainly the most developed in the field of the theory of international relations.[5]

De Magalhães argues for the necessity of "essential elements," "exact form," "clarified ideas," and "unmistaken notions" to be held firmly at hand when speaking or theorizing diplomacy. Otherwise, a theory that is founded upon "confused" notions and ideas is bound to lead us astray. But he also admits to the difficulties of reaching consensus, which has not been forthcoming following the protestations of Harold Nicolson over diplomacy's terminological confusion.

Nicolson's case is interesting in itself. Nicolson, in the first chapter of his *Diplomacy,* makes a considerable effort to clarify his terms and define his problematic. He points out that "in current language this word 'diplomacy' is carelessly taken to denote several quite different things," employed as a synonym for "foreign policy," "negotiation," "the processes and machinery of negotiation," "foreign service," and "tact."[6] Nicolson suggests that the indiscriminate use of these terms exposes the theme of diplomacy to "such confusion of thought" (4). In order to clear away the confusion, Nicolson proposes the employment of the *Oxford English Dictionary* (*OED*) definition of *diplomacy*, quoting as follows: "Diplomacy is the management of international relations by negotiation; the method by which these relations are adjusted and managed by ambassadors and envoys; the business or art of the diplomatist" (5). This quotation, however, is more interesting for what it excludes than for what it

says. For Nicolson does not fully quote the *OED* but uses only the
first subheading. He leaves out three subheadings:

2. The diplomatic body ([obsolete]).
3. Skill or address in the management of relations of any kind;
artful management in dealing with others.
4. DIPLOMATIC ([rare]). [The science of diplomas.]

Nicolson's attempt to delineate the proper theme of diplomacy is
consequently an exclusionary process dressed as a rational thematization that rhetorically resorts to the commonsense definition of the
dictionary—only that the dictionary entry he advises us to adopt is
not taken fully at its word. Even here there is confusion that again
needs to be clarified and conventionally managed. Nicolson's thematization is therefore selective, associating diplomacy with statecraft,
a view apparently confirmed by his own personal experience of
diplomacy as a professional diplomat in the British Foreign Service.

Such purifying and exclusionary processes for thematizing diplomacy are not peculiar to these two authors. They are typical of positivist analysis that through definitions attempts to delimit boundaries of thematic control and seeks to determine a stable subject
matter available for scientific study. But disciplinarian boundaries
are porous, and the subject matter is neither pure nor stable. Note in
this respect, just as another example, the debate of whether war is
the opposite of or forms a thematic part of diplomacy. On the one
hand, R. B. Mowat argues that "war is the negation of diplomacy,
which means contact without arms."[7] Similarly, a nineteenth-century
play, quoted by William Roosen informs:

For an intelligent man, is there anything more absurd than war? And
by its very nature isn't war the born enemy of diplomacy? What ob-
jection can you make to a hundred thousand bayonettes and what argument can oppose a cannon shot? War is the misuse of power, the
triumph of force; where the saber reigns thought is mute and civilisa-
tion exists no longer. . . . But, when in the silence of an office, a man
using only the influence of reason in happy and skillful combinations
is able to put a limit on ambition, to maintain equilibrium and peace
between the different powers, and to force men to be happy in spite
of themselves without taking up arms and without spilling their
blood, that!, that is something which cannot be admired too much;

that is something beautiful, something sublime. It is the triumph and the work of genius![8]

To this diplomacy-war opposition, one can contrast Carl von Clausewitz's notion of war as "the continuation of policy by other means,"[9] or Thomas Schelling's "diplomacy of violence,"[10] or the "coercive/ gunboat diplomacy" of many others,[11] or William Rogers's definition: "Diplomacy is the art of saying 'nice doggie' until you can find a rock."[12] In other words, conventional diplomatic literature equally includes and excludes war as a theme of diplomacy—something that prompts one to think how the theme gets thematized.

THINKING AS HANDICRAFT

In his 1951–52 lecture series Heidegger points to the craft of the hand to explain the act of thinking:

> The craft of the hand is richer than we commonly imagine. The hand does not only grasp and catch, or push and pull. The hand reaches and extends, receives and welcomes—and not just things: the hand extends itself, and receives its own welcome in the hands of others. The hand holds. The hand carries. The hand designs and signs, presumably because man is a sign. Two hands fold into one, a gesture meant to carry man into the great oneness. The hand is all this, and this is the true handicraft. Everything is rooted here that is commonly known as handicraft, and commonly we go no further. But the hand's gestures run everywhere through language, in their most perfect purity precisely when man speaks by being silent. And only when man speaks, does he think—not the other way around that metaphysics still believes. Every motion of the hand in every one of its works carries itself through the element of thinking, every bearing of the hand bears itself in that element. All the work of the hand is rooted in thinking. Therefore, thinking is man's simplest, and for that reason hardest, handiwork, if it would be accomplished at its proper time.[13]

This peculiar passage on the philosophy of the hand raises, I think, a number of interesting issues. First is the claim that the craft of the hand enjoys a special position in the act of thinking. In fact, Heidegger specifically makes the point that thinking is a handiwork, the simplest and hardest. Second, Heidegger reverses the metaphysical position that thinking precedes speaking: "And only when man speaks, does he think—not the other way around that metaphysics still believes." Language, in other words, comes before and is, in fact, a prerequisite for thinking. But the manifestation of language, Heidegger argues elsewhere, requires the inscription of the hand, as handwriting: "The word as what is inscribed and what appears to the regard is the written word, i.e., script. And the word as script is handwriting."[14] Handwriting, the manual inscription of signs, is important for Heidegger because it is this very act that first gives food for thought and is therefore most thought-provoking. That is why he wishes to preserve handicraft and argues against modern typographic mechanization, which degrades the word and reduces it "to a simple means of transport, to the instrument of commerce and communication."[15]

To that extent, Heidegger maintains that the handiwork involved in writing is not and should not be treated as insignificant. There is a certain primal praxis in the writing (*graphein*) of letters (*grammata*) that needs to be retrieved and safeguarded. This praxis at the level of inscription is what Derrida later radicalizes in his *Of Grammatology*, that is, not only that speaking precedes thinking but also that writing precedes speaking.[16] Handiwork is important for actively reflecting on the Being of entities, and that is in the way words as tools or equipment are given assignments. It is in the everyday dealings and manipulations of things that we discover their manifold assignments (that is, what word works, how it works, why this word and not a different one) and not in a detached theoretical grasping of things. This practical behavior toward things, their everyday handling, Heidegger calls "readiness-to-hand," contrasting it to the theoretical behavior that holds and takes things as "present-at-hand."[17] But it is important to note here that the terms *handling* and *readiness-to-hand*, by interpolating practice into what is considered sovereign theoretical territory, also seek to surpass conventional theory-practice formulations of thinking and what is involved in it.

Thinking cannot be disassociated from the thing it thinks. But what it thinks is itself what is put to question in thematizing diplomacy. If thinking is a handicraft, and if the study of diplomacy is also peculiarly linked to the study of handwriting, then one ought to consider not only how diplomacy can be rethought in terms of handicraft but also how thinking can be rethought in terms of diplomatic practice—to show, in other words, how thinking involves duplicity (double writing, double reading) and truth-making (contextualization, delineation of interpretive boundaries and communities).

Handicraft is implicated both in the thinking of diplomacy and in the diplomacy of thinking.

To that extent, thematizing does not first posit the entities but instead allows their interrogation at the level of inscription.[18] Note that a theme does not only relate to a subject or topic of thinking; it also refers to a stem or root of a word, "the part of which inflections are added" (*OED* definition). In other words, diplomacy can be thematized also by breaking up its word, by dividing it into themes. Indeed, Heidegger suggests that "the breaking up of the word is the true step back on the way of thinking."[19] Thus the proposition that follows the breaking up of the word, diplo-ma-cy, is that at least three other diplomatic themes can be recovered: that of the diploma, of the diplo/double, and of the diplomatic. The coup de main is a means of both giving voice to and rethinking these other themes.[20]

A SHORT HISTORY OF HANDLING

Although the word [diplomacy] has been in the English language for no more than two centuries, it has suffered from misuse and confusion.
—Satow's Guide to Diplomatic Practice

Handling, that is, a lightness of pencil that implies great practice.
—SIR JOSHUA REYNOLDS, *quoted in the* Oxford English Dictionary

In *Satow's Guide to Diplomatic Practice* the continuity of a long diplomatic tradition seems to be secured for the faithful not only through historical accounts and exemplarity but also, interestingly, through the assumption that words are simple messengers in the service of a great profession: "Diplomatists existed long before the words were employed to denote the class."[21] The same applies to diplomacy by implication: namely, that it existed before the word was first used to denote it. For it was known by a different word, and before that by a different word, and before that by a different word. Was diplomacy known to have existed without a word? Is this possible? Could an entity be ready-to-hand or present-at-hand outside language? Could one separate the concept from the word that describes it, the word that brings it into presence? Saussurian linguistics suggest that thing/word and signified/signifier are two sides of the same coin, and post-Saussurian linguistics indicate the interplay of signifiers in search of a signified, thus the importance of etymology for retheorizing diplomacy. Diplomatic themes, to that extent, cannot only be recovered in the exhaustive readings of a certain evolutionary history of diplomacy as traditionally pursued but also in the history or career of the word *diplomacy* itself.

The use of the word *diplomacy* can be traced back only as far as the late eighteenth century. Dealing with the thematics of the term, an 1877 entry on diplomacy in *Encyclopedia Britannica* states: "It is singular that a term of so much practical importance in politics and history should be so recent in its adoption that it is not to be found in Johnson's dictionary."[22] Etymologically, however, the word is derived from the ancient Greek verb *diploun* (to double), and from the Greek noun *diploma,* which refers to an official document written on double leaves (*diploo*) joined together and folded (*diplono*).[23] In the first instance, such ancient diplomas written on parchment and on papyrus were handed over to heralds carried as evidence of their status and authority. The word *diploma* in extended use "came to mean a letter of recommendation, especially of the nature of a passport; and later, an order enabling a traveller to use the public post."[24] This meaning of the word *diploma* as an official paper conferring certain rights on the bearer entered into classical Latin through Cicero, Seneca, Tacitus, Pliny, Suetonius, and others.[25] During the Roman Empire, for example, diplomas were called "all passports, passes along imperial roads and way-bills stamped on double metal plates, folded and sewn together in a particular manner."[26] Later, in early medieval times, "this word 'diploma' was extended to cover other less metallic official documents, especially those conferring privileges or embodying arrangements with foreign communities or tribes."[27]

It is important to note, however, that during the above-mentioned period no word with the roots *diplo-* or *diploma-* was used by either the ancient Greeks or the Romans to describe instruments and representations of statecraft currently designated by the term *diplomacy* (the Greek word *diplomatia* is only found in modern Greek). Instead, in ancient Greece the most commonly used word was *presbeia* to denote the sending of an embassy, a word that also referred to the state of being old (*presbeis*) and, during the Christian era, to the priesthood (*presbutairoi*). Other words employed were *theoria* for missions to oracles and religious festivals, *angelein* for the sending of messengers, and *kerixein* for heraldry. The Latin word used by the Romans for the sending of an embassy was *legatio,* a word that had a number of other meanings. The word *legatus* could be used inter-changeably to mean an envoy, a government representative, a gover-nor of a province, and a deputy or lieutenant general. Later, the word *legatio* was also employed in Medieval Papal representation for temporal as well as for ecclesiastical representation.[28] In other words, there was no single term that conveyed the themes of diplo-macy in terms of statecraft, deputation, negotiation, foreign policy, tact, and so on, nor was there a word that could be simply used as a substitute for the term *diplomacy* without any supplementary politi-cal associations and meanings.

During the late medieval period, nonetheless, there was a use of the word *diploma* in something reminiscent of a diplomatic sense. For instance, Alexander Neckam of St. Albans in a poetic survey of nature, *De Laudibus Divinae Sapientiae*, wrote around the begin-ning of the thirteenth century:

> Praetendens faciem plenam terrore minaci in venatoris obvius arma ruit: sed cum luminibus sese subduxerit hostis, utile jam censet esse diploma sibi [Showing a face full of threatening terror, he rushes for-ward to meet the weapons of the hunter, but when he comes face to face with his enemy, he now thinks that cleverness/stealth/devious-ness/intelligence (*diploma*) is useful to him].[29]

As Stephen Gaselee suggests, this particular use of the word *diploma* "has clearly the meaning of a diplomatic device or subtlety, and fore-casts the future use of *diplomacy* in English."[30] If one accepts this proposition, then *diploma* appears to carry "diplomatic" meanings much before (four centuries earlier) the actual use of the term *diplo-macy*—meanings that have been lost and no longer carried with the single word *diploma*.

But these are not the only associations of *diploma* with the term *diplomacy*. By the sixteenth century, the Latin word *diploma* was systematically used to describe any papal letter of appointment to a mission. The word *diplomatarius* was subsequently attested to the chancery scribe in charge of writing out such *diploma*.[31] During the seventeenth century a further significant development took place that associated *diploma* with *diplomatica*.

The landmark of this development appears to have started with the charging of a Jesuit member of the Bollandist commission, Daniel Van Papenbroeck, with the examination of ancient monastic diplomas in order to determine their authenticity; their falsity had been suspected since medieval times. In his publication *Acta Sanctorum* (Acts of the Saints, 1675) Papenbroeck claimed that almost all Merovingian diplomas and other medieval documents were forgeries. This was a terrible blow to a number of monasteries, particularly those of the Benedictine Order, that maintained piles of ecclesiastical documents in their libraries. The Benedictines subsequently charged Jean Mabillon, a monk of the scholarly Benedictine congregation of St. Maur, with the task of refuting the Jesuit's declarations by pointing to the scientific flaws of his work. Mabillon published a book with the results and fundamental principles on the science of verifying documents under the historic title, *De Re Diplomatica* (1681). His methods for the study of the form, not the content, of old diplomas were subsequently accepted even by Papenbroeck, thus in effect constituting the foundations of the new diplomatic science.

Of particular interest is not only the title of the book but also the structure of the diplomatic material in it. Mabillon divided the diplomas under examination according to the century and the type of script. Chronologically, the samples of scripts dating from the fourth to the thirteenth century were easy to arrange. But with regard to the type of script, Mabillon categorized the different types "'Gothica,' 'Langobardica,' 'Saxonica,' and 'Francogallica' in isolation from one another as national scripts of the Germanic peoples and set them apart from Roman handwriting."[32] This decision to classify types of script by nationality is a crucial one, for it meant that the scientific study of handwriting, known as *diplomatica,* was considered capable of separating, say, Germanic from Roman writing and Germanic from Roman hands. Even in writing the same language, Latin, the hands of the scribes were proposed as having distinctive national features and techniques of writing. Thus the nationcentric features of *diplomatica* were suggested despite the fact that the so-called national scriptoria were employing scribes from different European nations; that was especially the case with religious and monastic scriptoria that Mabillon was primarily investigating.

Later, Scipione Maffei of Verona refuted Mabillon's claim of the so-called national type of script, arguing that all national types were developments of the Roman one and thereby dividing the Latin script into "majuscule," "minuscule," and "cursive." Nonetheless, the "inter-national" character of *diplomatica* did not disappear, for it was associated with the "outstanding paleographical achievements" of that period.[33] For purposes of examination, diplomas continued to be divided on national lines. This practice was followed by Gottfried Leibniz, who gathered the original texts of important public documents and treaties from the eleventh to the fifteenth century and published them in a book, *Codex Juris Gentium Diplomaticus* (1695), although this time, significantly, *diplomatica* was employed for purposes of studying the content rather than the form of diplomas.

More publications followed in the eighteenth century, like the momentous six-volume publication *Nouveau traité de diplomatique* (1750–65) by the Maurist Benedictines, René-Prosper Tassin, and Charles-François Toustain, completing and extending Mabillon's thesis by incorporating things like church and royal sigillography. This book also appears to have introduced *diplomatique* as the French equivalent of the Latin *diplomaticus* and, of course, of the English *diplomatic(k)*. Parallel developments were also taking place in the use and meaning of *diploma* and *diplomaticus*. Dumont, the Emperor's historiographer, published the *Corps universel diplomatique du droit de gens* (1726), which contained the original texts of "the Treaties of Alliance, of Peace, and of Commerce, from the Peace of Munster to 1709." In the case of Dumont, consequently, just as in the case of Leibniz, the meaning of *diplomaticus* as the study of diplomas shifted from form and handwriting to the subject matter deposited in the writings of particular collections of *diplomas*. This resulted in equating *diplomaticus/diplomatique* with the study of *droit de gens* and by that associating it to the study and knowledge that concerned relations between kings and states—no longer just the study of handicraft but the knowledge of statecraft. In other words, *diplomatica* was increasingly paying more attention to the different political styles and effects of authorial sovereignty and less to the hand of the scribe and the acts of handwriting that produced the material or *diploma*.

Alexander Ostrower summarizes this linguistic development to *diplomatica* and subsequently *diplomatie:*

> Towards the end of the eighteenth century the word "diploma" had undergone a process of transformation resulting from its specific usage in the political terminology of international relations. The

meaning of the word shifted from the form of the document to its contents, from the paper itself to what it actually represented in international relations. The new word *diplomatie* (diplomacy) thus derived signified the art or business of the *diplomarius* of the French *diplomate*, and the English *diplomatist*, or *diplomat* by contraction. Thus diplomacy had become the craft of a person entrusted with an official mission by a state in its intercourse with other countries. . . .

Increased political activity created the need for a new approach to official communication, and the old *diplomes* authorizing representation were replaced by the *diplomatie*, the new method of intercourse, and the *diplomate*, the representative of a state.[34]

To consider this shift of emphasis compare, for example, two diplomatic entries from 1780, the former dealing with the study of diplomas in general, the latter with diplomas linked to international relations in particular. First: "a diplomatic description was not so much required in that letter, as I had directed my attention more to the contents of the book than its external appearance," in which *diplomatic* refers to the careful examination of the diploma for purposes of authentication.[35] And second: "These were followed, at due interval, and according to all the established rules of form, by measured and regular discharge of the *diplomatique* artillery on all sides [that is, manifestos and declarations by the French and Spanish governments]," in which *diplomatique* refers to the conduct of international relations through the exchange of diplomas.[36] Seven years later in the same journal, the *Annual Register,* the word *diplomatique* was repeated with an IR tinge to it: "Employed there in civil, *diplomatique*, and mercantile affairs."[37]

The link of the diplomatic with diplomas and handwriting was increasingly overshadowed by the newly established political theme. In 1796, one comes across Edmund Burke's writings and the first (according to the OED) recorded use of the word *diplomacy*. A somehow reluctant entry, not in the main text but as a footnote, reads: "It may be right to do justice to Louis XVI. He did what he could to destroy the double diplomacy of France. He had all the secret correspondence burnt, except one piece."[38]

By the late eighteenth century, therefore, and after a long linguistic journey (through *diploa, diplomas,* and *diplomatics*), the word *diplomacy* acquires a particular political thematization attached to statecraft and external affairs. Hence the crafted word is registered in dictionaries, attached to another chain of words that purport to explain and mean it. Needless to say, these explanatory words remain open themselves to the same hermeneutical process.

But this is not the end of the story of handling. Stabilizing the meaning of *diplomacy* requires constant policing. Historical (etymological, grammatical, phonetic) associations with the signifier may be tolerated, and sometimes even acknowledged, but their significance has to remain subservient to the disciplinarian interpretation. Other senses must be held in check in the name of sense, of common sense, of diplomatic common sense.

A good illustration of this process is provided by Stephen Gaselee's short genealogical story of the word *diplomacy*. In a book titled *The Language of Diplomacy*, Gaselee engages in what appears to be an otherwise useful introduction to the etymology and other potential meanings of the word. But Gaselee is also very keen to suppress those other senses he so laboriously worked to uncover. He seeks to tie *diplomacy* to an exclusively political theme, a domain of inquiry that can be confidently described and analyzed. Thus Gaselee urges: "Let us here rid ourselves once and for all of the other use of the word 'diplomatic.'"[39] On meeting some lexical resistance, he wishes for a form of linguistic cleansing: "Such use of the word *diplomatic* still exists, though tenuously, and I could wish that it would wholly disappear" (12). And after the linguistic extermination, catharsis is declared: "All this is to clear away what might be a misleading side-meaning of the word now under examination. We can now return to 'diplomacy' in the ordinary modern sense of the word, with its adjective 'diplomatic'" (13).

All these rituals of thematic sublimation are not unique to Gaselee, though not often stated so explicitly. They form part of a more general rationalization scheme working under the illusion of a perfectly representational thought. In the case of Harold Nicolson, the exclusionary process is more tactful in the sense that the study of diplomas and handwriting is initially fully acknowledged as an integral part of diplomatic history:

> As these treaties accumulated, the imperial archives became encumbered with innumerable little documents folded and endorsed in a particular manner. It was found necessary to employ trained clerks to index, decipher and preserve these documents. Hence the profession

of archivist arose, and with it the science of paleography—the science, that is, of verifying and deciphering ancient documents. These two occupations were, until late seventeenth century, called "*res diplomatica*" or "diplomatic business," namely the business of dealing with archives and diplomas.

We do not always realize the importance acquired during the Middle Ages by the collection and the orderly arrangement of archives.[40]

But Nicolson's reasoning is still colonialist in the way that these practices are valued for their service to statecraft. Thus the diplomatic-paleographic science is now given technical expression in the "diplomacy" of contemporary interstate contacts that deals with "the preservation of archives" and "the analysis of past treaties":

This scientific, this scholarly element is still vital to the functioning of any efficient Foreign Service. The British Foreign Service, for instance, possesses in its Treaty Department a body of specialists upon diplomatic procedure, in its Library a highly competent staff of experts in precedent, and in its Legal Advisers a group of technicians steeped in the niceties of treaty-drafting and international law. Without such a staff of historical and legal experts precedents would be overlooked and inaccuracies might be committed. It is thus important to emphasize what might be called the scholarly or technical origins of diplomatic practice. (12)

The theme of diplomacy associated with handwriting and the regulation of diplomas has, according to Nicolson, developed into an upgraded scholarly, historical, and legal expertise in interstate relations. Handicraft forms part of, and is now totally subservient to, statecraft.

DIPLOMACY AND ITS DOUBLE

So far I have suggested that the theme of diplomacy could be illustrated not only in statecraft but also in handicraft, that is, in the inscription, arrangement, and authentication of diplomas. This is so because diplomacy owes its name to this association with diplomas, a denomination that also ties diplomacy to the science of diplomatics. For once the distinction between word and thing, nominal and real, is problematized, one can no longer dissociate the process of crafting the sign of diplomacy from the theoretical or conceptual

construction of it. In the etymological thematics of diploma, therefore, the theme of diplomacy gets rewritten, reread, and redefined.

But diplomacy as primarily a handicraft means that it also involves the crafts of the double hand, the process of doubling. The
thematization of the word *diplomacy* recovers a double theme, that
is to say, the doubling of authority and sovereignty that comes with
the double mace of diplo-macy.[41] *Mace* means the herald's or messenger's staff that represents authority, authorizing the agent as an official medium, *missus* being actually the name for the royal procurator
in the Carolingian period.[42] *Mace* also denotes the scepter of sovereignty: "My murdring Uncle . . . that longed for my Kingdome and
my Mace."[43] Consequently, in English diplo-macy but also in French
diplo-matie and Italian *diplo-mazia,* one can read the doubling of
the mace and the representative's *sceptrum clava.*

If diplomacy is, however, both statecraft and handicraft, then the
doubling of the mace involves not just the duplication of political
sovereignty but also of authorial sovereignty. The act of doubling
confers on the writing of diplomacy the sign of sovereign presence,
authorizing the inscription to re-present the concept, treating the latter as present-at-hand. The word *diplomacy* becomes the double of
an absent concept, the way an ambassador appears as the double of
a sovereign. But note still that the diplomatic language associated
with statecraft engages in particular forms of duplication and
economies of duplicity. For "the essence of good diplomatic drafting
is, where possible, to avoid saying anything that admits of only one
meaning."[44] This duplicitous writing expected of the professional
diplomat, however, may be characteristic also of the writer of diplomacy. In fact, I go as far as to argue that these duplicitous crafts figure in the writings of the first craftsman of diplomacy (accepting for
a moment the evidence of the *OED* that designates Edmund Burke
as the first known user of the word *diplomacy,* though the general
proposition here is neither dependent on this specific individual
being the first nor on the existence of an original scribe). Could it be
then that the craftsman inscribed diplomacy with a double hand and
a double meaning?

In 1796, Burke writes in a footnote: "It may be right to do justice
to Louis XVI. He did what he could to destroy the double diplomacy
of France."[45] Let us reflect for a moment on the implications of what
is being said here. Burke speaks of "double diplomacy." The first

time diplomacy was given to us, it took the form of a double. In presenting us with this gift, Burke issues a warning concerning its form and status: this particular diplomacy is not the one, the first, the original but, rather, the double, the double diplomacy, the double *of* diplomacy.[46] This is because double diplomacy was not the official diplomacy of France, but the "secret," "perplexed," "dark," "evil," and "false" diplomacy that was practiced in parallel to the official one during the reign of Louis XV.[47] And yet it seems that it was so authorized, indeed initiated, by the king himself. It involved "the administration of a curious system" through which the king with the help of a few trusted envoys engaged in secret diplomacy behind the backs of his ministers. In other words, it was officially authorized by the sovereign diplomatic authority in whose name diplomacy was practiced. It was officially decided to be unofficial. This double diplomacy was, so to speak, officially unofficial and unofficially official. Why then all this fuss from the craftsman of diplomacy? Why all this effort to denigrate the double?

Was double diplomacy any less authoritative? In many ways, quite the opposite. It was more authoritative for it was communicating the wishes of the sovereign in whose name diplomacy was practiced. This ingenious scheme was after all the means through which the king chose to authorize his representations and inscribe his sovereignty. Of course, this duplicitous authorization of the king's policy meant in effect that there was not "one court in which an ambassador resided on the part of the ministers, in which another, as a spy on him, did not reside on the part of the King."[48] Furthermore, it meant that it was common for an inferior to the French ambassador who nonetheless received secret instructions from the king to engage in his own negotiations and so to effectively "checkmate the negotiations of his superior, without the least suspicion on his part of the disloyalty practised upon him."[49] Still it was conducted under the auspices of sovereignty.

Was the problem of double diplomacy then its secrecy and duplicity, as Burke seems to imply: "What is truly astonishing, the partisans of those two opposite systems were at once prevalent, and at once employed, and in the very transaction, the one ostensibly, the other secretly, during the latter part of the reign of Louis XV" (281). But secrecy and duplicity in diplomatic affairs—between sovereigns as well as within the administration responsible for the practice of diplomacy—was not anything uncommon during that period, as it is not uncommon today. In his *Secret Diplomacy* Marx had a lot to say about such acts of duplicity, and for that matter, the Kissinger "back-channel" diplomacy or the Irangate events provide recent examples of this same practice. Why then specifically criticize double diplomacy, unless one is prepared to pass moral judgment on the practice of diplomacy as a whole?

Could it be perhaps that the problem of double diplomacy was of a more practical nature, having to do with the confusing double instructions, the double writing involved in the preparation of dispatches, and the double reading required of those who tried to understand and respond to it? There are indeed a number of examples of the diplomatic confusion created by Louis XV's duplicity. One of his secret envoys, Chevalier Douglas, in his first attempt to contact the Russian Empress in 1755 failed precisely by being too secretive about his role. He posed as a simple tourist, "carrying with him a snuff-box with a *double bottom* in which his instructions and itinerary were concealed," and his attempt to approach the Empress through the British ambassador was treated with suspicion.[50] In this mission, so the legend has it, he was accompanied by Chevalier d'Eon de Beaumont who was disguised as a woman.[51] It is therefore easy to argue the complicating effects of double diplomacy, for only a year later Douglas succeeded in having an audience when he returned fully accredited and with d'Eon as his secretary. Note, however, that d'Eon, who finally took over the double diplomacy with Russia, on this occasion "had been supplied with a copy of the *Esprit de Lois* with a *double binding* in which were concealed letters to the Empress and ciphers for the correspondence of the rulers behind the back of their Ministers and Ambassadors"—a sign of the king's preference for double, rather than single, dealings.[52]

The issue of double writing is additionally exhibited in d'Eon's double reports: "*Two sets of reports were dispatched*, one to the Foreign Office, the others through Tercier to Conti and the King."[53] Consequently, French diplomacy also involved a double reading by those envoys who were at the same time employed both officially and unofficially. In the case of the double envoy there was the problem that he was presented with the task of remaining faithful to two sets of instructions. There was always a double reading of the instructions he received (everything read with a double eye and with regard to the secret wishes of the king). But in order to remain faithful to the French Ministry (and formally to his king), the double ambassador also had to pursue a certain policy in public, while at the same time undermining it in private. Inevitably, the court he was accredited to also had to engage in a double reading of its own.

Nevertheless, this craft of double writing and reading in the practice of French secret diplomacy is not absent from Burke's own representations of diplomacy. Burke also engages in duplicitous writing, sending two messages at the same time and accrediting more than one representation with the same word-messenger. This appears, for example, in Burke's use of the term *corps diplomatique* in the following two quotations. On the one hand, one could read the words as referring to the body of literature on foreign affairs (the early understanding of *diplomatique*); on the other hand, one could take them in terms of the corporate body of ministers:

> All this body of old conventions, composing the vast and voluminous collection called the *corps diplomatique*, forms the code or statute law, as the methodised reasonings of the great publicists and jurists from the digest and jurisprudence of the Christian world. In these treasures are to be found the *usual* relations of peace and amity in civilised Europe. [54]

> The Prussian ministers in foreign courts have talked the most democratic language. The whole corps diplomatique, with very few exceptions, leans that way. [55]

The same duplicity applies to Burke's use of the words *diplomatic* and *diplomacy*. They are presented to us with double credentials, sometimes to convey the association with diplomas and diplomatics and at other times to convey the work of statecraft. In the *First Letter on a Regicide Peace*, Burke speaks of "the diplomatic collection" in terms of a deposit of national diplomas, but also of "a diplomatic curiosity" concerning governmental policy (259, 215). Moreover, in the *Fourth Letter on a Regicide Peace*, Burke gives this new term *diplomacy* yet a different sense, denoting a group of foreign envoys: "The foreign ministers were ordered to attend at this investiture of the Directory. . . . The diplomacy, who were a sort of strangers, were quite awe-struck with 'the pride, pomp, and circumstance' of this majestic senate" (73). This other meaning of diplomacy conveyed by

Burke is now obsolete. But Burke's uses of the words *diplomacy* and *diplomatique* as diplomatic corps or depository of diplomas constitute an aberration and an exception only to the extent that diplomacy as statecraft is the normal theme—that is, only within the thematic propriety of the discipline. Burke's writings register not only diplomacy or double diplomacy but inevitably also Burke's double hand, which in turn prompts our own double reading of his diplomacies. The king's duplication is, therefore, not different from Burke's duplication. Duplicity is as characteristic of the diplomatic practitioner as it is for the diplomatic writer. Burke's inscription of diplomacy is done in a manner that is peculiar to the diplomatic craft.

THE THEMATIC DUPLICITY OF DIPLOMACY

Conduct which is wily and subtle, without being directly false or fraudulent, is styled diplomatic.—An 1877 *definition of* diplomatic, *the* Oxford English Dictionary

The writing of diplomacy involves the craft of the double hand. Its reading is therefore neither single nor final. This view constitutes nothing new or original to the practitioners of diplomacy, who engage in their own duplicities, passing two (or more) messages simultaneously, reading between the lines, reading what cannot be seen. That is why it would indeed seem very strange, and utterly undiplomatic, to insist that a theory of diplomacy should reach a single or final reading of what diplomacy is or what diplomacy entails.

To that extent, duplicity should not be seen simply as a negative practice or a useful diplomatic technique.[56] When it comes to the theorization of diplomacy, duplicity could refer to the double-citedness of the text, the "plurality of readings that underlies double reading [and] is not equivalent to arbitrariness, but is understood positively in terms of the dissemination of the text."[57] Diplomacy provides therefore a *pour parler*, a duologue, a dialogue of readings, and a juxtaposition of writings that cannot foreclose but leave open the reinscription of thematic borders. The thematic duplicity of diplomacy projects its own ethics of dissemination that could suggest a different approach to world politics, not as a world of universally enshrined, self-evident truths but one that constantly involves truth-making.

That truth constitutes a theme of diplomacy—as suggested both by the rhetoric of diplomatic practice and the authenticating science of diplomatics—has important implications for the true theme of diplomacy. What does this tell us, in other words, about the possibility of such a true theme, when the rhetoric or bestowal of truth is implicated in the very diplomatic theme it seeks to delineate? This is not just to point to the possibility of deceit, evasion, or economies of truth that are characteristic of diplomatic discourse and that thus need to be acknowledged and taken into account when diplomatic themes are advanced. More significant, and perhaps more suggestive, the thematic duplicity proposed above indicates the need to investigate the condition of truth, and the truth of truth. Even Sir Henry Wotton's famous definition of the ambassador as "an honest man sent abroad to lie for the good of his country" is fundamentally based on such a discourse of truth, for an ambassador can only lie truthfully! The possibility of truth is already presupposed in deviating from it. As Lacan underlines: "Even if it communicates nothing, the discourse represents the existence of communication; even if it denies the evidence, it affirms that speech constitutes truth; even if it intends to deceive, the discourse speculates on faith in testimony."[58]

The true theme of diplomacy, therefore, cannot avoid confronting the question of truth and truth-making. That is not simply the metaphysical understanding of truth as likeness and correspondence but also the originary conception of it as unconcealment and disclosure (*a-letheia*). It is important to note here that among the early Greek thinkers *aletheia* was just another word for Being, the way *theoria* is taken in the writings of Plato to be a particular manifestation and experience of Being. There is, to that extent, an originary interdependence between theoria and *aletheia*. As Heidegger says, "that the basic Greek experience of being is *theoria* does not testify first and foremost to the priority of seeing and looking but testifies above all to the primordial holding sway of the essence of *aletheia*, in which there dwells something like the clearing, the lighted, and the open."[59]

Theoria is not simply a way of establishing an ideational relation to theory or diplomacy. It indicates, rather, the positing of that relation to the opening of truth-making. Before the contemplative, theoretical relation, the acts of *aletheia* clear and illuminate the space where diplomacy stands, appears, and is completed as the thing that it is. The true theme of diplomacy, therefore, always refers back to the opening of the true; put differently, it refers back to the opening of the path of theoria, which is the clearing path of thinking.

THEAMA

protocol

The term "protocol" comes from Greek words meaning "the first glue," and indeed it may be said that protocol is the glue which holds official life in our society together.—MARY McCAFFREE and PAULINE INNIS, Protocol: The Complete Handbook of Diplomatic, Official and Social Usage

Diplomacy, Theater, and the Other

The specialist role played by the spectacle is that of a spokesman for all other activities, a sort of diplomatic representative of hierarchical society at its own court, and the source of the only discourse which that society allows itself to hear.—GUY DEBORD, The Society of the Spectacle

Our greatest need reflects our gravest danger: until we learn how to recognize ourselves as the Other, we shall be in danger and we shall be in need of diplomacy.—JAMES DER DERIAN, On Diplomacy

The momentous diplomatic events and breakthroughs that preceded the end of the Cold War were nowhere better dramatized than in the summits of the superpowers. These carefully orchestrated meetings designed precisely for their impact, attracted high media attention combined with "deep" political analysis of the televised moods, expressions, and tactics of the two parties. Although few doubt the importance of the spectacle, particularly its capacity to move the negotiations further and reverse decades of mobilized hostility, hardly anybody could have imagined the revelations of who the most influential person had been: Nancy's astrologer! Two officials of the Reagan administration, Donald Regan, the National Security Adviser, and Larry Speakes, the White House spokesman, underlined in their memoirs the astrologer's influence on President Reagan, something that the Reagans never denied. This was followed by the astrologer's own book, which offered breathtaking accounts of how she single-handedly changed Reagan's negative perception of Gorbachev and how she was involved in timing or confirming the Geneva, Reykjavík, Washington, and Moscow summits, as well as planning the actual length of negotiations between the two leaders. In the same book, there is finally a fascinating astrological interpretation of why the Intermediate-range Nuclear Forces Treaty is currently unsafe because the astrologer's demanding advice was not followed to the last detail.[1]

Perhaps more important than the question of why Reagan's horoscope should be relevant to superpower summit diplomacy is the question why not? Why is it that the astrological text is generally deemed an other of diplomacy? Why is it that contemporary political imaginary cannot cope with horoscopic explanations, can no longer look at the stars for political signs? These are not just rhetorical questions. A brief historical look is enough to illustrate how in ancient times astrology was a fundamental instrument for guidance in the realm of political and external affairs. In their palaces, Babylonian kings and Egyptian pharaohs kept royal astrologers, priests expert in the divination of the stars and their occult influence. The role of the prophet-astrologer was further mentioned by Kautilya in *Arthashastra*. In ancient India,

> astrologers extended solid support to political authority. They proclaimed the divinity of the king in battles and held out prospects of sure victory to his soldiers. For the start of his conquests Harsa's astrologers fixed such an auspicious day and lagna as would ensure his victory in all the four quarters. They could prevent political upheavals and popular commotions by predicting evil consequences for their sponsors.[2]

For the ancient Greeks the political reading of celestial constellations was also important. Homer emphasized the role of the soothsayers in the Trojan expedition. Spartan military action could be taken only during a full moon, and following an eclipse of the moon the Athenian Nicias, "who was rather over-inclined to divination of such things," did not engage in negotiations "until they had waited for the thrice nine days recommended by the soothsayers."[3] In short, the view that astrology historically formed a significant aspect of politico-diplomatic action seems well founded.

That is why it would be too quick a response to dismiss Reagan's horoscopic dependence in discharging his diplomatic functions as yet another of his anecdotal peculiarities. For there is something in the practice of modern diplomacy that precedes the normal staging of superpower summits: namely, the staging of diplomacy we have become accustomed to—a staging in which astrological participation seems currently at odds with the proper performance of the diplomatic.

In this chapter, consequently, I want to consider how theatrics constitute not simply the ceremonial role of diplomacy, but a protocol, a first-glue role that recognizes the dramatic aspect as an effective part of the *techne* of diplomacy. I investigate first the relationship between theater, theory, and diplomacy. I then move to examine the fictions that sustain diplomacy as a distinctive political performance. Finally, I look at the staging of the other for the production of diplomatic subjects and objects.

DIPLOMACY, THEATER, AND THEORY

*Illustrissimi regum et rerum publicarum legati in mundi nunc theatro
. . . congregati [Most illustrious ambassadors of kings and states, gathered
before the theater of the world.]*—JOHN AMOS COMENIUS, Angelus
Pacis ad Legatos Pacis

Theatrical presentation offers an innovative—though not unprecedented—way of thinking about world politics and diplomacy. In a recent text gathering the different voices of IR theory, James Rosenau resorts to theatrical genre to consider the debate and has this to say about "the pleasures of drama": "The context of drama enlivens the mind, lifts the spirit, and in the process the writer derives the pleasure of creativity, of knowing that one is moving below the surface and encountering the core of experience and the stark realities within which choices must be made."[4] But beyond this deeply personal experience, there is also a more direct link between theater, theory, and diplomacy.

Recent IR literature has sought to expose the relationship between these three concepts.[5] In *Theatre of Power*, for example, Raymond Cohen sets out a project for explaining diplomatic contacts in terms of dramatic presentation. The first chapter, titled "Diplomacy as Theatre," is an exposition of how diplomats constantly find themselves on public stage and so always obliged to assume prearranged roles in the official diplomatic play. By restricting his theatrical interpretation, however, to nonverbal signaling, like posture, facial expression, body movement, dress, and so on, Cohen's thesis poses some serious problems.[6] Cohen ignores the constitutive role of language by approaching the theatrical form of communication as extralinguistic. But language is of the utmost importance in theater—that is, how through linguistic means, such as the act of naming, an object attains its reality on stage. To suggest that theatrical forms are somehow outside or beyond the realm of language is to miss the point that posture or dress have language written all over them, including body language, and that diplomatic theatrics can make sense only when situated in political discourse. By limiting his theatrical application to nonverbal acts, Cohen is able to make some witty comments about the presentational tricks diplomats employ when on show, but he fails to provide anything like a theorization of diplomacy as theater.

It is important to note, however, the extent to which the theoretical text is implicated in the theatrical one. As shown in the previous chapter, the etymology of *theatron* can be traced back to *thea* and *orao*, which points to the link between spectacle (*theama*) and theoria, in terms of view, eyeing and watching something attentively for a long time. Theoria as philosophical act is not foreign to *theama*. Platonic theory is narrated through metaphors of vision, its knowledge acquired through privileged philosophical views (ideas). Philosophy is claimed by Plato to be in its essence wonder-working, miraculous, and thaumaturgic. Put differently, philosophy is of the spectacular kind, of the empathic viewing encountered in the theater: "For this feeling [*pathos*] of wonder [*thaumazein*] shows that you are a philosopher, since wonder is the only beginning/principle [*arche*] of philosophy, and he who said that Iris was the child of Thaumas made a good genealogy."[7] Not only is this passion of the spectacle the cause of philosophy, but Plato once again seems to implicate this spectacular viewing with the early forms of diplomacy. Note that Iris, who is one of the god-messengers, is claimed to have originated from *thauma* (wonder).[8] In thaumaturgy, spectacle, philosophical thinking, and diplomacy are again integrated.

Further links between theater and theoria can be found in Aristotelian works. Aristotle follows Plato in arguing that philosophy as theoretical science (*episteme theoretike*) begins with wonder: "Wondering [*thaumazein*] in the first place at obvious perplexities, and then by gradual progression raising questions about greater matters."[9] Theoria, just like theater, is cathartic (*he theoria katharsin mallon dunatai*).[10] In the *Poetics* Aristotle speaks of a wrong theory (in the play *Odysseus the False Messenger*) in terms of misperceived theater (*ek paralogismou tou theatrou*).[11] Finally, from a different perspective, the success of any dramatic plot depends on good theorization (*theorousi to en kai to olon ek tes theorias*).[12]

In ancient Greece, consequently, *theatron* was a medium of critique and self-reflectiveness. As J. Peter Euben argues:

> Drama was also a theoretical act and institution in the sense that the theater was an occasion, place, and way for theoretical considerations to become relevant to practical affairs without violating the contingency and irony of action. This was possible because the citizen audience became simultaneously spectators and actors. As spectators of the action in the play they could see a whole denied to those who enact their parts and who were therefore bound to the particular. But as political actors they could take part in a whole they can only partially know, thus imitating the actors on stage. This double vision is the foundation for Aeschylus's view that suffering brings wisdom and wisdom suffering, of Sophoclean irony, and for Socrates's dictum that ignorance is the foundation of knowledge. It is also a reason why tragedy has been called "the epistemological form par excellence."[13]

Ancient Greek tragedy dealt with philosophical issues like the status of knowledge in decision-making (*Oedipus Tyrannos*) or the manipulation of democracy through sophistry and demagogy (*Bacchae*). The ancient Greeks theorized in theater as much as they dramatized theory in the Platonic cave. They did so within the ambit of the affairs of the polis—in other words, within the ambit of the arena of the political.

To that extent, theater enjoyed a pedagogic status as with philosophy. Both were viewed and theorized, the former on stage (*epi skenes*) and the latter at the marketplace (*eis ten agora*) or in the Academy. But theater also had a public, political role to play, as Euben explains:

> Tragedy was a public event and a political institution. It was performed before and for the public, largely by the public, and judged by citizens it helped to educate to the task of judgement. Because plays were public events, their meanings, unlike those of our own plays, were interjected into the polis itself through the context of performance and festival. For the duration of that festival the city turned

itself into a theater watching itself as an object of representation at stage. (51)

This turning of the polis into a political theater, and so of politics into dramatic performance, is further illustrated in the content of the highly political tragedies of Aeschylus, Euripides, and Sophocles and the political comedies of Aristophanes. In other words, *theatron*, in dealing with the affairs of the polis was not merely a political instrument but was actually inseparable from ancient Greek political process. According to Euben, *theatron* has little in common with modern professional theater:

> For us drama is a literary genre or form of entertainment that we choose from an array of recreational opportunities. The choice itself is thought to have no political or moral dimensions but to be simply a matter of individual preference. Nor is drama a collective experience beyond the moment of performance. We enter and leave theater as strangers. Any bond created by the experience of the play is a temporarily shared suffering fractured at the play's end. (50)

The contemporary politicization of theater is done more in terms of the artistic expression of a political ideology or agenda (from George Bernard Shaw to Václav Havel) or the study of politics behind play production.[14] Interesting works that offer insights into the general understanding of theater through politics and vice versa cannot claim for the theater the privileged political role it enjoyed in ancient Greece, that is, its indistinguishability from the very political action it dramatized.[15]

Yet there was also a specific relationship between *theatron* and the diplomatic practices of theoria. This can be seen primarily in the functions of the theoric fund (*theorikon*). This public fund, established by the Athenians through the collection of city revenues, subsidized theatrical performances, and during the period of Pericles it was also used to pay for poor citizens to attend them. The theoric fund was, however, also the fund that paid for the sending of the city's sacred ambassadors to shrines and religious festivals.[16] It was charged, therefore, with the expenses of both the *theatron* and the theoric embassy:

> Even though part of the expense of the *theoria* . . . was shifted to the *architheorus*, for the *architheoria* was a liturgy, and in fact one of the most expensive, considerable sums were nevertheless left to be paid

by the state. Further the state was obliged to maintain the state ships, Paralus and Salaminia, which were chiefly intended for such purposes and were on this account called the "sacred ships."[17]

The theoric fund was consequently in charge of two types of inter-linked performances: the first dealt with the staging of theatrical per-formances, and the second concerned the staging of diplomatic ones. For the purposes of *theorikon*—subsidizing the production and con-sumption of spectacles—theater, politics, and diplomacy are treated as a unity.

There is also another sense in which theater is linked to theoria. For it was in the Dionysian celebrations, where theorias were sent from almost all other city-states, that the first dramatic contests were introduced in the sixth century B.C.[18] From this it could be deduced that the theoric ambassadors were also the first theatrical actors. A search into etymology could point to the word *skene* meaning hut or tent, which was the place where the *theoroi* dwelt on their theoric expeditions, but it was also the word used to denote the dramatic stage. In *skene* (or scene), therefore, the dwelling of the ambassadors of theoria becomes the political and aesthetic space accommodating theatrical performances. Later, with the construction of permanent theaters, an altar *(thymele)* to Dionysus was built at the site so as to discharge the necessary religious rituals previously fulfilled by the theoric embassy. The citizens, actors, and spectators became then the new theors sent on a private theoria to the *theatron*. Going to the theater was in every sense like participating in a theoria, for such "places of performance were usually connected with the sacred precincts of the gods."[19]

Theatron was therefore a medium through which the Greeks were taken on a mental flight, given a theoretical overview of their political life. But *theatron* was also an internal embassy, a politicized space where the polis waged a drama for itself and its citizens and of-fered political and politicizing representations of itself.

Later, the techniques of dramatic performance were hierarchically incorporated in the service of Byzantine policy. During this period, however, theater lost its critical function and became subservient to the imperium, in the way the political and diplomatic scene was carefully orchestrated for narrating the story and glory of the em-pire. Note, for example, how the palace staged the reception of foreign embassies. The foreign envoys were welcomed at the borders and escorted to Constantinople via the longest and worst roads (to create the impression of inaccessibility). Once in the capital, they were accommodated in a palace that served as a comfortable jail. Nothing was left to chance, for the envoys could go out only with their "honorary guard" and were prevented from approaching ordinary people. The military might of Byzantium was then presented in never-ending parades in which "the same troops, emerging from one of the gates and leaving by another, came round and round again carrying different types of armour."[20] The envoys were also shown the impenetrable walls of Constantinople, its impressive churches, and buildings.

The long-awaited procession and reception by the emperor was the most spectacular. Bishop Luitpart described the stunning reception of his embassy by Nicephorus Phocas. In front of the emperor's throne, there was a golden tree surrounded by rare birds, flying and singing. On the two sides of the throne, there were two golden mechanical lions that made terrible noises. Following Byzantine etiquette, Luitpart made his submissive bow, but by the time he raised his head, the emperor was elevated high up to the ceiling, like a deus ex machina, and wore a different costume.[21]

Theater as a courtly spectacle gets subsequently institutionalized in late Medieval and Renaissance courts: "Luxurious court theatres were built, to display the taste and patronage of some monarch, prince or duke."[22] Permanent courts refined the aggressive spectacle developed by Byzantine diplomacy by staging a new drama where resident envoys were not only spectators but actors, participating in dances, processions, masques, and other performances. During this period, diplomacy could thus be explained better as a theater of power than as a traditional balance-of-power system.[23] Inevitably, such performances proved also to be a site of dramatic contestation. Ceremonial details and precedence had to be properly performed with the utmost care and sensitivity.[24]

In the contemporary age of high-tech media, a main characteristic of diplomatic practice is the pluralization and privatization of stages. It no longer involves simply an official spectacle centered on the sovereign and produced by accredited agents. In an age of prolific and instantaneous reproduction of global images directed from different sources, diplomatic representation is caught in the web of mass-media networks. Late-modern diplomacy thus engages in its own war of spectacles. As illustrated in James Der Derian's reading of the Gulf War, the battle of diplomatic representation in the media network had to be won first before the allies could proceed to the actual military operation, which itself engaged in new manipulations of the war spectacle.[25] To that extent, the shift of stages, the new media, and the new politicized actors provide additional challenges to the theorization of diplomacy as a sovereign political performance.

OF DIPLOMATIC FICTIONS

Fictio figura veritatis [Fiction is the figure of truth].—ST. AUGUSTINE OF HIPPO

I have argued that the structure of modern diplomacy is both the structure of Western metaphysical thought and the structure of representation. But the diplomatic structure also depends on fictions that narrate and sustain it as a distinctive political performance. These fictions of diplomacy are enacted through a process that involves dramaturgy: that is, the determination of a space of action; the anagnorisis, the identification of politicized subjects and objects; the development of a plot. In this global drama, the suspension of disbelief and the forgetting of fictions are a prerequisite for entering the staged illusion. But in contrast to the theater, the fictions and the dramas of diplomacy never end. Its fictional dramas attain a life and logic of their own: they become the world of diplomacy, they are what there is.[26] The capacity to maintain this metaphysical space, to direct this global stage and to continuously sustain its fictions is what the *techne* of diplomacy is also about.

I intend to deal in this section with what I term the four fundamental fictions of diplomacy—fictions that establish diplomacy as real on stage. I consider these fictions to be minimal prerequisites (though not exhaustive of the list of IR fictions), the essentializing ground (*fundamentum*) for an official diplomatic performance and so foundational in the fullest sense. It is fiction, then, not merely as negative illusion but also as a creative, productive faculty for the staging of diplomacy.

The Fiction of the Sovereign Subject

This fiction of the sovereign subject conventionally refers in the modern era to the territorial state as the main dramatis persona of world politics. Francis Hinsley reminds us that "the state—or at

least the instrument of power to which we should apply this term—
exists in the phenomenal world."[27] This is perhaps the point at issue.
How does the state exist as a phenomenon, as a thing that appears,
and what are the effects of such an apparition? It is important to
note here that the most sophisticated authors tend to resist the temp-
tation of restrictively defining the origin or end of this phenomenon.
Jean-Jacques Rousseau, for example, maintained that "the sovereign, by virtue of what it is, is always that it ought to be."[28] And Yah-
weh, the other sovereign, addresses Moses's wonder before the mission to Egypt in the most provocative way: "I AM that I am. Tell
them that I AM has sent you to them. . . . This is my name for ever.
This is my title in every generation" (Exodus 3:14–15).

Indeed, a number of political theorists argued that the condition
of sovereign statehood exemplifies many of the features of the
Judeo-Christian God.[29] According to Carl Schmitt and Karl Löwith,
for example, the state is the effect of secularized theological concepts
that appear in God's multiple identities: eternal, absolute, legislative,
policing, and welfare powers.[30] State, then, is the eternal subject, the
one that speaks diplomacy eternally (not Vichy's France but Charles
de Gaulle's *France Éternelle*).[31] It is a state that writes command-
ments, signs covenants, and binds itself to the future; a subject that
takes it upon itself to spiritually redeem its followers and physically
protect but also punish them in doing so; a state that seeks to gov-
ern, regulate, and administer all things in its realm, that is, an
almighty holder (*pantokrator*). But this omnipotent sovereign can
exist only in its omnipresence, presented in its iconic representations
(names, maps, flags, emblems, crowns, institutions, and so on). In
short, the state has to be stated.[32] What I gesture toward here is a
short genealogy of fictions that constitute the miracle of enacted
statehood. It is particularly evident in the Latin articulations of state
and sovereign, such as *Deus in terra, imitatio Deus, vicarius Deus* or
*vicarius Christi, corpus mysticum, lex animata, persona personalis et
ideali, persona et res publica, persona ficta.*[33]

In conventional IR theory and practice, this fiction is further extended by attaching a will to the state. The state thereby becomes a
subject, an autonomous, independent, and sovereign persona that
wills. Thus, it has obligations, rights, and interests. It is said to be capable of feeling secure, insecure, and threatened, and capable also of
committing violations, aggressions, and injustices. It can be held

responsible and liable, and it must communicate, decide, and be aware. In short, it is treated as having human as well as divine attributes.

Note an example, finally, of how an IR theorist gets arrested by this fiction, to the extent that it brands the state with a "concrete physical existence":

> The important point to note is that all these formal states, whose governments take part in the ritual quadrille of international diplomacy . . . actually exist: they can be located on the map; they have more or less defined boundaries; they have settled populations and identifiable social and political institutions.[34]

The actuality of the representations of this notional entity (state) is here neatly taken for the actuality of its existence, a fiction turned into a reality, with a life and logic of its own.

The Fiction of the Representative Agent

The sovereign subjects engage in diplomatic intercourse through their accredited agents. In agency, therefore, one deals with the need of establishing the fiction of working representation, that is, how the sovereign subject voices its word and makes known its will. Accrediting the agent may take different forms, ranging from the luminous wreath of the angel, the royal ring of carrier pigeons, or the staff of the messenger to the declaratory letter bearing the signs and seals of sovereignty.

It is characteristic of the need of multiple levels of representation that Medieval Papal practices developed different degrees (and fictions) of diplomatic agency according to the situation. The *vicarii*, for example, usually chosen from the residential bishops, were entrusted with permanent missions and had the capacity to stand in the pope's place and officially act for him. Not only did they act in his name but they made his presence felt (*suas vices*), for those to whom the *vicarii* were sent were instructed to see in their face the pope's own face and in their voice the pope's own voice (*ut propriam faciem nostram sen nostrae vivae vocis oracula*). The *vicarius* was therefore a *vicarius Papa*, but the pope was also a *vicarius Deus*, which meant that the actions of this particular agent also represented the will of the divine sovereign.

The *legati a latere*, however, did not possess the same authority to establish the full presence of the pope. They were sent *a latere* (literally, from the side of the pope, *ex latere nostro*), and so only part of the pope's authority was represented in their actions. The *legati nati* represented the temporal authority born (*natus*) out of the pope, while the *legati perpetui* were vested with the power to represent universally and permanently. The *legati missi* were simply sent, and their authority was that of a living letter dispatched by the pope. The *apocrisarii*, finally, were permanent representatives in foreign courts, particularly to the one in Constantinople, that were merely given the authority to answer (*apokrinontai*) for the pope.

All these forms of papal representation were later amalgamated in the office of the apostolic nuncio, who in the beginning was a representative dealing with administrative and economic matters such as the collection of taxes. The apostolic nuncio subsequently assumed the highest diplomatic office, sent to negotiate the pope's own affairs and those of the Holy See (*pro nonnullis nostris atque Sanctae Sedis negotiis*). As to the office of the ambassador, it constituted the lowest form of representation and was only used for the menial jobs of the Holy See (*ambactus,* being a servant). It was only after the 1268 Venetian decree that the office of the *ambaxiator* acquired the high official status it currently enjoys.[35]

These different forms of representation established, therefore, different fictions of agency, which were later extended to cover secular diplomatic practice, such as the *plena potestas*, which gave the representative full powers to act in the name of the sovereign subject in negotiations and in the signing of treaties. Furthermore, there was the secularized medieval fiction of transmutation, relating to the theological *homoousion* ("the Father and I are one"; John 10:30), where the legate was supposed to carry inside him the body of the king: "Thus he was transmuted from the King's representative into the very King himself—a mystery which occurred wherever the ambassador appeared in state."[36] Finally, note the concept of exterritoriality where the diplomatic agent by legal fiction was regarded to be outside the territory of the state to which he was accredited (beyond the reach of the territorial sovereign). The idea that the body of the legate was *ex territorium,* a notion that transcended terrestrial space and time, was thus analogous to the corporeal attributes of the celestial intermediaries, the angels who lacked any material presence but assumed physical characteristics such as face or body.[37] In modern diplomatic discourse, the new argument of "functional necessity" is now put forward for the justification of privileges and immunities—the contemporary rational argument, as if the functions of the diplomatic missions are any less fictitious. This last point is illustrated by the following two fictions.

The Fiction of the Instrumental Object

Diplomacy is dominated by the system of objects and signs that constitute its everyday life. This system of objects must be arranged, organized, and manipulated in ways functional to the technical discourse of diplomacy. The objects' value for signification, however, is not inherent but invested in them. The third fiction of diplomacy, therefore, refers to how diplomats, engaging in a practice of symbolic exchange, simultaneously project identifications and meanings on otherwise neutral objects. An object acquires instrumental value when one bestows on it special features, qualities, and attributes that it otherwise lacks.

Take as an example a table employed as an object of diplomacy. It is not merely seen in conventional social terms as an object that can be eaten on, written on, play cards at, and so on. In diplomacy it is also used as an instrument of bilateral or multilateral negotiation. The shape of the table or the arrangement of separate tables is consequently considered significant and, at times, controversial, for it determines the type of negotiation—or the status of the participants: for example, the long rectangular table for bilateral negotiations; the semicircle or horseshoe tables for conference diplomacy; the square table to indicate equality of status; the T-shaped table adopted in the recent Middle East negotiations in Madrid; the Π-shaped table suitable for official dinners; the round table that elides the questions of identity and status; the empty table that registers official participation but also symbolic absence of some party from the negotiating process; and finally the "super-ellipse" table invented by the mathematician Pief Hein to meet the high demands and complicated six-month deliberations between the different parties in the Paris negotiations on Vietnam.[38] The point of the table as an instrumental object of diplomacy is precisely the capacity to infer from its form and shape the presence of status and policy. This is achieved by attaching meanings to the otherwise unimportant physical qualities of the table, that is, the imaginary projection of signification by means of overdetermined interpretations.

The premises of the embassy provide another illustration. Just like the diplomat, the embassy is rendered inviolable, a rule developed from the legal fiction of exterritoriality (that is, that the premises of it belonged to the territory of the sending state). As such, the space where the embassy resides is objectified in instrumental ways that elevate it to an extraordinary topos, a house of "earthly gods," which is like a temple open to asylum seekers.

These technical processes of instrumental objectification apply to many other diplomatic sites including, for example, the different types of diplomatic correspondence (note, *note-verbale*, nonpaper, and the like) and the different kinds of diplomatic agreement (treaty, memorandum of understanding, and so on). The object of diplomacy is consequently an effect of signification, inscribed with political value and meaning.

The Fiction of the Specialized Process

Finally, we arrive at how diplomacy becomes what diplomacy is, how diplomacy is identified as an autonomous concept, a totality that carries with it a whole history and a whole political world. The concept of diplomacy seems to be secured through an ordinary but fundamental assumption that constitutes its culminating fiction: namely, that it is something different, that it involves a domain of experience that is distinctive.

Imagine diplomacy then. Attempt a totalizing image of the diplomatic process perhaps in the very familiar—now regularly televised —form of two persons sitting comfortably, smiling at each other, and talking politely. One may wonder what is so special about this, what is so peculiar that can render this process diplomatic. Is it the status of each person? Is it the capacity in which they talk? Is it the content of what they say? Is it the spatial and temporal circumstances of the meeting and the talking? Can we distinguish in the final analysis what diplomacy is, and what diplomacy is not?

Try the following elaboration. The king of France sits on a sofa smiling and talking to the duchess of Savoy about affairs of state (diplomacy). The king of France sits on a sofa smiling and talking to his mistress about their love (not diplomacy). At this particular moment in what appears to be the same act, the way that the king of

France regulates his relations with the duchess of Savoy on the one hand, and with his mistress on the other, differs only to the extent that in the first case he is acting in his diplomatic capacity (as a political subjectivity), whereas in the second case he is acting in his capacity as a lover (as a sexual subjectivity). If his mistress also happens to be the duchess of Savoy, however, then there is no distinction at all. What takes place is a double, undifferentiated mediation. Their diplomatic relations become indistinguishable from their sexual relations. He is having intercourse with her natural but also with her political body. And the satisfaction he offers her, and vice versa, can be translated into diplomatic influence. What makes the act different, diplomatic or nondiplomatic, is the bestowal of particular identities on the participants. It is also interesting to note how diplomats precisely engage in such manipulations of diplomatic presence/absence. Examples of this point include "boudoir diplomacy," such as Lord Malmesbury's mission to St. Petersburg to seduce and induce Empress Catherine into an alliance, when the empress flirted for an alliance both with the ambassador (sexually) and with his king (politically).[39] With this in mind the medieval ambassador was advised never to be accompanied by his wife, "lest she be suborned."[40] Finally, this compounding of different states of subjectivity that were mediated at different levels explicitly concerns the notion of marriage diplomacy, which was common in European interdynastic relations.

But the idea of the specialized diplomatic process has been constantly challenged by professional transgressors of diplomacy who deliberately offend against conventional practices and instructions. They often register their countersigns in a way that also enacts a parody of the whole diplomatic process: examples include the antiprotocols of Idi Amin Dada carried triumphant on the shoulders of four British diplomats; Emperor Jean-Bedel Bokasa's imitating Napoleon's coronation process to the last detail; or Colonel Mu'ammar al-Gadhafi's setting up his bedouin tent, surrounded by six camels and bereted lady bodyguards, outside the Non-Aligned conference hall in Belgrade. These "political transvestites" and their traverses of the process of diplomacy parade diplomatic theatricality to excess and so provide "a celebrated temporary liberation from the prevailing truth and from the established order."[41] Through their exaggerated mimicry, they make a mockery of the official dramaturgy of diplomacy by exceeding the limits of the serious and proper and so taking diplomacy to its ultimate, carnivalesque extent.

STAGING THE OTHER

We are engaged in an orgy of discovery, exploration and "invention" of the Other.—JEAN BAUDRILLARD, The Transparency of Evil

The relationship between diplomacy and the discourse of otherness has been directly addressed in the writings of James Der Derian. *On Diplomacy* is a pioneering work that attempts to devalue the accepted truth of diplomacy and expose the theoretical presuppositions on which it is founded. Der Derian suggests that diplomacy has neither "an essence of common sense," as Nicolson argues, nor "an origin that can be chronologically and geographically fixed."[42] Instead, diplomacy is an ensemble of practices, power struggles, and truth contestations that develop into a dominant discourse for dealing with the other. Der Derian consequently approaches diplomacy as the mediation of estrangement, the "mediation of estranged individuals, groups or entities," or in its modern incarnation, "the mediation of estranged peoples organized in states which interact in a system" (6, 42). By employing the terms *alienation* and *estrangement* Der Derian suggests diplomacy as an answer to the state of mind that has been historically constructed in different moments of consciousness and processes of knowing the world, a state where (human) subjectivity loses its "reality" by being compelled to derive existence out of processes of objectification rather than an inner self. In this stage of alienation, man denaturalizes himself. He becomes an object, the object of himself, and so finds truth and value outside himself. He becomes something other than what he really is. He becomes a means to an end that is not his own, thus the need of diplomacy to mediate the products of this alienated consciousness (from territorial states to different states of being). Diplomatic culture is identified as "the mediation of estrangement by symbolic power and social constraints" (42). Thus in this genealogical study of diplomacy, Der Derian suggests different "paradigms" interpretive of different discourses (also corresponding to different epochs) of diplomatic practice ("mytho-diplomacy," "proto-diplomacy," "diplomacy," "anti-diplomacy," "neo-diplomacy," "techno-diplomacy"). By providing various forms of diplomatic process and different ways of staging the other, Der

Derian not only succeeds in freeing diplomacy from a state-executional practice conventionally chained to raison d'état and realpolitik, but he also accounts for transformations and transitional phases of its historical evolution, identified by classical scholars but not theoretically grounded.

This is a massive task in itself, and overall Der Derian manages the material well. There are two things, however, that I wish to point out and take issue with. First, by proposing a theorization of alienation through the works of Ludwig Feuerbach, Karl Marx, and Jean-Paul Sartre, Der Derian (though referring to some inadequacies of alienation for fully explaining diplomacy) tends to emphasize the repressive, dominating aspect of alienation (respectively, domination of man by gods, domination of man by matter, and domination of man by social praxis). This repressive aspect of alienation is carried over to his understanding of diplomacy's condition of possibility. Moreover, this suggests a natural state, an existential condition to which the alienated subject *can* and *must* presumably return.

My understanding of alienation is more in the sense of estrangement, as pointed out by Fred Dallmayr,[43] both of which terms Der Derian uses interchangeably. This reading understands estrangement in a constitutive sense, as the only way to self-realization, the only way for the production of subjectivity (one that takes into account the immanent alterity of subjectivity), but also as an essential part of the objectivization process, of the creation of beings. Identity requires difference and difference refers to our capacity to estrange, to make something strange, alien, other. In this process of estrangement lies diplomacy's realization. As also derived from Der Derian's different historical moments of diplomacy, it is precisely because the ground is unstable, because diplomacy is founded in radical alterity, that there is the possibility of identity and equally the impossibility of any stable identity for diplomacy.

Second, Der Derian does not take his provocative argument to its theoretical completion, which is, I think, the ultimate lack of clear differentiation between diplomacy and all other forms of political, social, religious, and legal mediation. All forms of mediation involve the interaction of alienated, artificial subjectivities. This includes diplomacy. If diplomacy is the mediation of estrangement, it must be compatible and examined in parallel to other intersubjective forms and relations. Thus, there is no reason why diplomacy should be any more special than the rest. Diplomacy occurs only (and this is a very big only) at the point where these subjectivities become politicized, and politicized to the extent of being capable or having the status of diplomatic relations. But the terms *political* and *diplomatic* are narrative accounts bestowed historically, through processes of inclusion and exclusion, on certain kinds of practices and not on others.[44] Therefore, these terms are themselves highly problematic as to how they attain their identity. Diplomacy is part of the discursive construction and constitution of the political (not just politicized but politicizing). As such, diplomacy attains its difference only in the act of naming, that is, the process of rendering it a distinguishable part of the performance of the political.

This performance involves the staging of the diplomatic other, different sites of otherness where diplomacy is located and acted on. In modernity, the other is realized in two ways. Although Tzvetan Todorov identifies the possibility of several degrees, we can settle with the two extremes: the other-as-subject and the other-as-object.[45] These are not natural realizations but deeply ingrained tendencies of modernity to realize the surrounding world in terms of subject-object division, in terms of initiator of action and passivity or stasis. It is in its subject-object capacity that the other becomes a being-in-the-world, whereas in its pure encounter it remains a being-beyond-the-world.[46] As subject or object the other is no longer an abstract figuration of alterity, but it becomes a sign configured in order to be known. Diplomacy is enacted and performed through these estranged yet known subjects and objects. Consequently, this encounter with the subject-object figuration of modernity places the other as fundamental not only to the theory of knowledge but also to the knowledge and theory of diplomacy.

The Other-as-Subject of Diplomacy

Modern diplomacy is primarily and constitutively intersubjective. It deals with relations between artificial subjects. It concerns the staging and mediation of these discrete, differentiated subjectivities. My first working hypothesis, therefore, is that diplomacy is the enacted regulation of relations between self and other(s). The other is essential for diplomacy because, obviously, one cannot have relations with oneself. It is impossible to communicate with what is already one, with an undivided unity. There is neither a reason nor a need to mediate what is same. Furthermore, knowledge of the other is essential for knowledge and construction of the self. As Rousseau says: "The body politic is forced to look outside itself in order to know itself; it depends on its whole environment and has to take an interest in everything that happens."[47] Diplomacy's raison d'être is therefore established only when there are boundaries for identity and when those boundaries of identity are crossed. Diplomacy's condition of possibility lies in identity/difference, but in the radical alterity of the other also lies diplomacy's impossibility of mediating final identities. Diplomatic history offers many examples, and the post-1989 changes in Eastern Europe and the former Soviet Union provide a recent exemplification of this point.

Because there can be no congress without subjectifying, we should investigate the narrative construction of subjectivity through the discourse of otherness that includes legal, theological, and personal attributes and rationales. In international legal terms, this construction of subjectivity can be illustrated in the concept of self-determination, as a condition for independent statehood. But what is self-determination other than a process of differentiation, which among other things takes place through diplomatic regulation and representation, political construction of identities (for example, nation-building), separation between what is domestic and what is foreign that must also, incidentally, be recognized by the other (de jure or de facto)? A change from "the subjection of people to alien subjugation" to rule by the same, that is, self-government and self-subjugation.[48] Thus a constant process of alienation (making alien) and estrangement (making strange) is in operation here, through which the identity of the self is reproduced, sustained, and redefined.

The creation of subjectivity is both the reason and the effect of diplomacy. Thus, a beginning of diplomacy can be traced back to the narratives of creation itself. The genealogy of diplomacy, as Der Derian suggests, is integral to Genesis: the creation of a finite subjectivity over and against an infinite one, out of an "Eternal Thou."[49] Genesis is the story of the origin of the caesura, the division or the separation that is the opening from which "mytho-diplomacy" is established. But one may argue that the originary invocation of "mytho-diplomacy" does not begin with the Fall of Adam and Eve from divine grace, as Der Derian proposes. It begins, rather, from the very act of the Creation of (human) subjectivity. Difference existed from the very beginning, though separation in the spiritual sense is a product of the Fall. For even in the Garden of Eden there was a distinction between Man/Woman and God, and the consequent need for regulating the relations between them. Hence, in the tree of knowledge we have a clause of paramount importance (the forbidden fruit) in respect to how these relations had to be conducted. The Fall drastically changed the circumstances and the ways of dealing with the other that had to be renegotiated and sealed with a covenant at Mount Sinai.

For modern purposes, it is interchangeably in the creation of life, subjectivity, or statehood that the conditions of diplomacy are currently to be found. The birth of subjectivity heralds the natality of diplomacy, a political conception and contraction of statehood that requires the political mediation of diplomacy. This natal aspect of subjectivity can be found, for example, as stated by the Trusteeship Council when the South Pacific island of Nauru was considered for a period to be in no sense a potential state, for it "cannot be regarded as a nation in embryo."[50]

Still, if we need to follow a natal logic, what is the other but the nonsensical environment the self encounters at birth? A new world that must be ordered, taught, interpreted, and made intelligible—in short, it is a world that needs to be mediated. The journey toward otherness: the journey from the womb down to the vagina and into a new semiotic *chora*, the semiotic universe every newborn discovers once it leaves the same, once it escapes the body of the mother. Note, for example, the official gift of the British colonial representative to the newly born state of Tuvalu on the day of independence: the *Shorter Oxford Dictionary*![51] Perhaps it is not just a sign of cultural arrogance but too appropriate and appreciative because a dictionary is a useful tool for translating otherness, mastering political polysemy, shaping the linguistic chaos awaiting the newborn island-state as it entered the international community. It was an introduction to learning the foreign language before it could assume a diplomatic role in the global play. Or, rather, the gift could be interpreted as a means of teaching the new state how to sign and authorize its discourse, how to become an author and an authoritative subject that properly binds itself with a sovereign signature: "If it gives birth to itself, as free and independent subject . . . this can hold only in the act of the signature."[52]

The story of diplomacy begins consequently when the umbilical cord is finally cut, when the somatic link is broken, when the newborn is effectively and irrevocably separated from the (m)other. The newborn subjectivity must establish a new link, a social one, to communicate with the mother, who is now an other. What was previously mediated biologically must now be mediated socially and politically. What was a purely internal relation must now become an external one. What was previously within the domestic domain must now become a foreign, interstate relation that requires the establishment of diplomatic relations with the metropolis, the opening up of embassies, the sending of missions and delegations. To that extent, the newborn is also charged to deal with all others that were previously mediated through the mother.

There is, I think, no better illustration of this compounding of human/individual and political/diplomatic identities than the case of Monaco. In this case, the state persona (enlivened) and the human persona (living) are integrated and become indistinguishable: for in the event of no (male) heir to the crown prince, Monaco loses its statehood and automatically comes under the sovereignty of France. The very existence of this state is guaranteed by the existence and sexuality of a single individual. If one were to take this provision to its extreme but logical conclusion, then one could imagine the possibility of a sterile or impotent head of state, or the situation of a transsexual heir, one who looks male but feels (or acts) female, or a transvestite who transgresses his sexual identity at will, or even a hermaphrodite whose sexual identity is infinitely ambiguous. Monaco could then become an entity of ambiguous political status. The sexy and sexist state of Monaco is therefore realized in the maleness, sexual state, and sexual appetite of its heir. This is not without precedence in political history, for the Great Khan also constituted his temporal power and empire in a sexual manner by violating six virgins every three days chosen from different parts of China.[53] In the global stage, the narratives of sexual performance and political performance cannot always maintain absolute distinctions.

But there is also another kind of subjectivity that we must trace in the self and its birth. It is not only the state but also its agent, the representative of the state that is also born in otherness. So enters the newborn or trainee diplomat into a new semiotic world, into unintelligible signs. At the same time watching and on stage, this is the world s/he must enter, animate and live in order to be constituted as a diplomat, become a chosen one. It is only in being inscribed by the signs of diplomacy, in disciplining the body to its rituals, rules, and protocols of civility that s/he can become a full member of the diplomatic corps.

The art of diplomacy involves a process of dealing with the other, with things new and different, just as in early childhood. Thus, the *fort-da* game where the child learns to distinguish and manage the presence/absence of his mother, has its own difficulties and complications as do multilateral negotiations on the Law of the Sea where the diplomat must learn how to identify the presence/absence of national interest. This problem is exemplified again in the case of the Republic of Nauru, which went as far as to advertise for a minister of external affairs in Australian newspapers, "offering a four-year contract in the first instance"—a dramatic call for a technocrat who understands the global plot and could take the leading role in this absurd performance.[54]

But the diplomat is also an other herself, for it is the fate of the representative always to be an other. Agency is pertained in heteronomy, not autonomy, for it invokes responsibility in the ethics of the other.[55] In her official capacity the diplomat exists only as representing the will of the sovereign and never her own. Jacques Lacan explains:

> What do diplomats do when they address one another? They simply exercise, in relation to one another, that function of being pure representatives and, above all, their own signification must not intervene. When diplomats are addressing one another, they are supposed to represent something whose signification, while constantly changing, is, beyond their own persons, France, Britain, etc. In the very exchange of views, each must record only what the other transmits in his pure function as signifier, he must not take into account what the other is, qua presence, as a man who is likable to a greater or lesser degree. Inter-psychology is an impurity in this exchange.[56]

Diplomats, therefore, continuously find themselves in and as the other. The determination of their diplomatic identity is always outside of them, that is, registered in the diplomatic passport, the excellency, the credentials, the diplomatic list, the rituals and ceremonies. Their diplomatic presence is recognized only in effectively representing themselves as diplomats. Thus, Fregozo, an envoy of the king of France, was put to death even though there was no mistake over his diplomatic profession, but being on the way to a secret mission to Constantinople he did not carry with him the letter of credence. His presence was not disputed (he was well known, and he was recognized for who he was), but his presence as a diplomat could not be officially or legally established.[57]

The other-as-subject involves, therefore, the determination of diplomatic subjectivities and the multiple faces or states these subjectivities may assume. The question of identity is, therefore, combined with the question of how subjectivities come to be known for what they are and what they do, and how theorists and practitioners are subjected to this form of knowledge that produces a particular regime of truth.

The Other-as-Object of Diplomacy

Turning now to the technologies for the production of the diplomatic object, my second working hypothesis is that diplomacy can exist only in the scene of the other. The locus of the other is the environment in which diplomacy evolves. Diplomacy has no mechanism for self-realization. Our awareness of it is not unmediated. The mediation of estrangement concerns alienated subjects but also the objects through which we make sense of relations and diplomacies. It is in this respect that realizing diplomacy, just like any other thing, stands beyond us but still involves a personal experience. As Cornelius Castoriadis notes, "my discourse must take the place of the discourse of the other, of a foreign discourse that is in me: speaking through myself."[58] For there is still "the continuous and continuously actualizable possibility of regarding, objectifying, setting at a distance, detaching and finally transforming the discourse of the other into the discourse of the subject."[59]

Consider the following semiotic *chora* and the interpretive process that may be required to move from the strange object to the familiar one. Among other things, it includes: bilateral and multilateral negotiations, concerts, conferences, assemblies, international institutions, specialized agencies, and good offices; legations, delegations, embassies, nunciatures, peoples' bureaus, exterritorial seats, and corps d'élite; balances of power, domino principles, peremptory norms *ius cogens*, *ex territorium* rules, raisons d'état, Kissinger models, and Sinatra doctrines; conventions, protocols, charters, treaties, unratified treaties, plain memorandums, and memorandums of understanding; declarations, denunciations, regulations, concordats, statutes, supplementary articles, general acts, *actes finals,* accessions, reservations, objections, interpretive statements, testimonals, expiry clauses, *rebus sic stantibus,* and terminations *stricto sensu;* corridor and gentlemen's agreements; communiqués, ultimatums, manifestos, proclamations, minutes, notes, *notes verbales,* collective notes, identical notes, dispatches, *lettres de cabinet, lettres de chancellerie, bouts de papier, pro memoriae,* and *aides-mémoires,* card indications (*pour remercier, pour faire connaissance, nouvel an, pour condoléances, pour presentation*); coups d'état, coups de théâtre, *coups d'éclat diplomatique,* esprits de corps, and *corps diplomatiques;* doyens of the *corps diplomatiques,* ambassadors extraordinary, ministers plenipotentiary, special envoys, *chargés d'affaires en titre* and *ad interim, legatus missus, legatus a latere,* and *legatus natus,* nuncios, pronuncios and internuncios, counselors, attachés and consuls; personae non grata, credentials, *plena potestas,* privileges and immunities (exception: *en flagrant délit*), diplomatic bags, pouches, or *valises diplomatique*s; couriers, ciphers and decipherers, hot lines, démarches, *compromis d'arbitrage,* and modi vivendi; ceremonies, protocols and etiquettes, decorations *boutonnière*s, full dress (*tenue de soirée*), *toasts d'honneur,* badges, and medals in miniature; excellencies, eminences, imperial majesties and royal highnesses, holinesses, monseigneurs, magnificences, venerables, and beatitudes; red carpets, military parades, gun salutes, anthems, exclusion corridors, and statues of unknown soldiers; flags, emblems, coats of arms, insignia, CD car plates, official anniversaries, national days, gastronomic tips, *vins de Saint Emilion,* fireside chats, cocktail parties, and cowboy barbecues; handshakes, smiles, and walk-outs; public statements, off-the-record positions, pregnant silences, acquiescences, no comments, confirmations, and denials—and both; trial balloons, tossed-salad approaches, genteel obfuscations, constructive ambiguities, and creative inertias; pompous acronyms, Latin clichés, Frenchified vocabularies, Levantine anecdotes, and Mandarin stories.

Not surprisingly, education in diplomacy requires a degree in *pansophia;* it involves the reading and writing of multiple signs and textual practices that are implicated in the diplomatic. The diplomat, therefore, is often seen or expected to be a person of letters, a bearer of mundane wisdom, a specialist of the general, and a polymath. Ottaviano Maggi speaks of the sixteenth-century envoy, a prodigy of learning, who should primarily be an expert of the heavenly signs:

> First of all, theology and sacred letters. Then all branches of secular knowledge: mathematics, including architecture and mechanical drawing, music, geometry, astronomy. The whole of philosophy, natural and moral, including, of course, a special mastery of the civil and the canon law, as well as of the municipal law and statutes both of his own country and of that to which he was assigned . . . [and] deeply read in literature.[60]

But the diplomat must also be an expert in *panlingua*—a multilinguist, a polyglot. Apart from the native language of the country to which he is sent, Maggi further requires of his envoy good knowledge of Greek and Latin and "all the principle modern languages, Italian, French, Spanish, German, even Turkish" (186). Nicephorus goes as far as to require of the ambassador "a knowledge . . . of all things and all languages"—all the possible ways, in short, of communicating with and through the other.[61]

That is why the early registers of *relazioni* were meant to construct a body of knowledge that would keep the agents of diplomacy "well informed and instructed concerning *all things*."[62] Francesco Antonibon describes what must be included in an ambassador's *relazioni*:

> It should describe the site of the province, giving both its ancient and modern names and its boundaries. Its subdivisions, its most important city, famous ports, fortresses, episcopal sees, principal rivers, mountains and forests should be described. One should treat of the climate, the temperature, rainfall, fertility, mines, animals. If the country is mountainous, forested, swampy, and if there is any noteworthy effect of nature, it should be reported. One ought to describe its inhabitants, their costumes, color, stature, disposition of mind and religion. The defences by land and by sea must be described. Their crafts and their commerce and the riches of both nobility and people should be included. Finally, the orator ought to come to the prince himself: his ancestry, person, life, customs, income and expenses, whether he is loved by his subjects, the guard that he maintains, the grandeur of his court, and with what princes he has friendship or enmity.[63]

And currently, an Institute for the Study of Diplomacy proposes that "any course in diplomacy, properly conceptualized, must present a synthesis of history and culture, political philosophies and systems, psychologies and ethical values, not to mention world geography and economic values and processes."[64] In contemporary practice, Angelos Vlahos found that even this was not enough. Questions for the entrance examinations to the Greek Diplomatic Service in the 1930s included: "How many times had Field Marshal Moltke smiled in his lifetime?" and "When did sharks first appear in the Mediterranean?"[65] Although initially Der Derian identifies *pansophia* with utopian thinkers and "anti-diplomacy," he points out that later, "with revolutionary zeal and secular ideas, Pansophism is reactivated to serve the neo-diplomacy."[66] Pansophism becomes necessary, therefore, to diplomatic practice, for knowledge of the signs of diplomacy presupposes knowledge of polysemy—the multiple signs through which the other may choose to appear. To manage the other is to be able to read and write the other, to produce and reproduce knowledge about it. In late modern diplomacy pansophism also turns into panopticism by means of spy and media satellites orbiting the globe, disseminating an ever-growing information frenzy.

There is, therefore, a process of objectification in diplomacy that situates the diplomat as a knower of diplomacy within a specific technology of manipulation and formation for the production of knowledge. In order to construct the diplomatic world, the diplomat must "discover resemblances as well as differences . . . self-knowledge develops through knowledge of the other."[67] The objectifying other is "both exterior to him and indispensable to him: in one sense, the shadow cast by man as he emerged in the field of knowledge; in another, the blind stain by which it is possible to know him."[68] The diplomat inevitably enters and performs this staged world—that is, s/he gets familiar with the meaning of signs, words, and practices, their correct and proper presentation, their usual or unusual order—so as to be able to engage in their artful manipulation and control.

THEON-ORA

hors d'oeuvre

An appetizer; out of the ordinary course of things [F. lit. "out-side the work"].—The Oxford English Dictionary

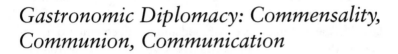

Gastronomic Diplomacy: Commensality, Communion, Communication

And I appoint unto you a kingdom, even as my Father appointed unto me, that ye may eat and drink at my table in my kingdom; and ye shall sit on thrones judging the twelve tribes of Israel. —LUKE 22:29–30

I fear our eyes are greater than our bellies, and that we have more curiosity than capacity.—MONTAIGNE, Of Cannibals

Dining is the soul of diplomacy.—LORD PALMERSTON

Social entertainment and official symposia have long been considered necessary for the smooth practice of diplomacy. There are numerous illustrations from diplomatic history on the political uses of food and drink, ranging from the habit of ambassadors always to take their own cook to avoid or instigate poisoning to mottoes such as Charles-Maurice de Talleyrand-Périgord's "Donnez-moi un chef, je me charge du reste." The dictates of gastronomy meant, for example, that in 1721 the retinue of the Ottoman envoy to the king of France included not only a chief cook, but also six kitchen aides, five caterers with two manservants, and a person especially charged to prepare the ambassador's Turkish coffee.[1] And currently, the foreign office guidelines point out to British diplomats that social entertainment is "one of the tools of our trade" and asks them "to be as scrupulous in this as we are in the performance of our other professional duties."[2]

Even though the importance of gastronomy is well registered in diplomatic practice, it is nonetheless conventionally approached as a dignified, not an effective, aspect of diplomacy. Consequently, there is a theoretical neglect of this issue, where at best one encounters simplistic, commonsense explanations of the political role of food and drink, that is, as a way to influence a diplomat or provide a comfortable working environment by means of edible delights and refreshing liquids. If we are to understand gastronomy simply as a natural or personal activity, or only as a socializing device, however, then we run the risk of leaving unexamined the political implications of it.

There are reasons why I think the politicization of gastronomy is a project worth pursuing. First, on a personal level, I was early on exposed to the multiple aspects of food and drink, coming from a region (the Mediterranean) and a country (Cyprus) where gastronomy constitutes an important part of social and political life, as a means of obliging, displaying favor, bonding, and assigning gender roles (women are largely responsible for daily culinary affairs, but men take charge during special festivities, for example, the Easter barbecue).[3] Second, the words *common, commensality, communion, community,* and *communication* were too etymologically suspect or too etymologically appealing to simply ignore. That is not only in English, but also in Latin and ancient Greek, as I show below. Third, there were already interesting works within other disciplines exploring the uses of food and drink. For example, in Freudian psychoanalysis, the totemic meal figures as a form of communication with the sacrificed deity as well as an unconscious commemoration, a catharsis from the original sin of patricide that follows the Oedipus complex.[4] Moreover, in cinematography the films of Bigas Luna magnificently pursue gastronomic metaphors in their examination of the link between sex, power, food, and drink (ham/penis, eggs/testicles, and milk/breast).

In this chapter I will sketch some illustrations from ancient Greece, the Bible, and modern gastronomic practices to suggest that gastronomy is not irrelevant or peripheral to political representation but, rather, that commensality and dietary practices are ways of inscribing community and feature forms of communication between parties in communion. In other words, gastronomy's importance lies, on the one hand, in its position as an investigating site of how community is produced in different historical and cultural spaces and, on the other, in the way it figures as a nonlogocentric form of communication. In pursuing this proposition, I work on the assumption that modern diplomacy—or the so-called dialogue between sovereign states—involves both a historically specific account of community and a theoretically determined rendition of global communication.

This is particularly so when one considers the *theon-ora* function of theoria. Theoria, being the most solemn of embassies, meant that it was not only relations between city-states that had to be mediated in classical Hellenic diplomacy, but also the relations between city-states and their gods. But note that theoria is also inextricably tied to the concept of theological gastronomy, something that Hans-Georg Gadamer identifies as the rationale behind theory's current inviolability and high status:

> Here we can recall the concept of sacral communion that lies behind the original Greek concept of *theoria*. *Theoros* means someone who takes part in a delegation to a festival. Such a person has no other distinction or function than to be there. Thus a *theoros* is a spectator in the proper sense of the word, since he participates in the solemn act through his presence at it and thus sacred law accords him a distinction: for example, inviolability.[5]

Theoria indicates, consequently, how the sacred table or religious symposium could confer on the participant the transcendental high ground associated with theory. It seems to me plausible to argue that theory, particularly as applied to diplomacy, should not only be linked to Platonic *theoria* (which is approached as an act of personal detachment, speculation, and philosophical contemplation), but also to this communal act that can establish theoretical/diplomatic truths through the consumption of religious commons during these solemn festivals. In other words, commensality could be taken to establish truths about the world, ways of collective seeing and nearness, ways of transmitting unity of thought and sharing, which Plato recognized in the Academy's symposia but left philosophically underdeveloped. For instance, in Plato's *Symposium* it is, after all, Agathon's banquet that prompts a philosophical meditation on love, where the participants in the discussion decide not to drink too much—to drink for pleasure and not to get drunk—as they were all suffering from a hangover caused by a symposium the previous night (note that Socrates is mentioned here as the company's stoutest drinker whose capacity overcame such trifles).[6] It is possible, in the end, that *in vino*

veritas could mean exactly what it says, especially if it is associated
with the incorporation of a sacrament that blesses the intoxicated ar-
ticulation with superior authority, for example, attached to the
Dionysian festivals where *theoroi* from all city-states were annually
dispatched. In short, the practice of gastronomy could register theoretical as well as political and diplomatic representation.

ANCIENT GREEK FORMS OF GASTRONOMIC DIPLOMACY

In *The Beginnings of Diplomacy*, an anthropological study that goes
back to the very basics of diplomacy, Ragnar Numelin provides an
abundance of examples of how feasts and drinking bouts were used
by tribal, nonhistorical communities as nonlogocentric means of
concluding or ratifying treaties. In the case of the Australian aborigi-
nes, the *corroborrees* (feasts) were employed for the resumption and
renewal of friendly relations but also as the only means for ratifying
a peace treaty.[7] For the conclusion of treaties among the African
tribes, Numelin gives an interesting illustration in the case of the
Masai: "Each tribe brings a cow with a calf and a woman with a
baby. The two calves are exchanged, and the enemy's child for that
of the Masai woman and the Masai baby is suckled at the breast of
the woman belonging to the enemy" (202–3). Among the "Congo
cannibals" treaties were ratified through drinking bouts of "sugar-
cane fermented liquors" (206). Finally, the drinking of blood by itself or mixed with food and wine was employed as a means of recon-
ciliation, for example, between the Papuans of New Guinea (207–8).

Gastronomic ceremonies, however, are not only a feature of tribal
communities or an aspect of so-called primitive communication but
also figure in the history of highly politicized units. In book II of *Politics*, for instance, Aristotle follows Plato to reemphasize the practice
of common meals. He stresses the sense of unity such common meals
created, especially in the case of Sparta and Crete.[8] Common meals
were used to create commonality, a bond of solidarity, like the one
found at the level of the family (because the family eats and drinks
together and so continuously reinforces its blood bond). The same
can be said of a group of families that share meals, as in a small vil-
lage community (a common practice in ancient Greece was, for example, the sharing of the same wet nurse—and the subsequent fra-
ternal and unbreakable bond of people who drank milk from the
same breast, *homogalaktoi*).[9] The point for Aristotle, therefore, con-

cerned the task of transferring this solidarity created by commensality at the micropolitical level of the familial community to the level of the polis, the political community.

Another important function of gastronomy, proposed in the *Nicomachean Ethics,* is its capacity to distinguish temperance (*sophrosune*) from profligacy (*akolasia*). The use of the gastronomic metaphor here is significant because temperance is associated to *phronesis* (reasonableness or practical wisdom), a foundational guide to how politics should be practiced according to Aristotle. The temperate, thus good citizen, is the one who is neither "a gourmand (*opsophagos*) wishing that his throat might be longer than a crane's" nor a "mad-belly" (*gastrimargos*) that eats and drinks beyond the right amount or natural desire.[10] In Aristotle's gastronomical ethics one discerns, consequently, a principle of politicization in terms of abstemiousness.

In the polis, it was indeed both a duty and an important function of the politicized citizen to participate in the commons (*ta koina*). This included participation in sacrifices, feasts, symposia where the citizens ate and drank together. The word *koinoneo* had precisely the meaning of participation in things common, as in the communal act of eating and drinking.[11] Greek *koinoneo* and Latin *communis* are currently translated by the English word *commune,* a word that itself entails the idea of conversing, of bringing together, of intimate intercourse, and also of eating and drinking in common or sacred meals. To that extent, every polis was understood by Aristotle as a *koinonia* (*pasan polin oromen koinonian*), and specifically as a *koinonia politike,* a political community.[12] For it was precisely in its communal aspects (the most natural of bonds) that the polis achieved its highest form of naturalization and unity and could subsequently speak with one voice, speak of its public interest and common good. It was on this communal aspect that political intercourse and communication was based, that is, in the act of sharing, exchanging a thing held in common.[13] By incorporating in common, the polis could itself become a corporation, a body politic. It was in the act of commensality and its politicization, therefore, that the ancient Greeks originarily also communed and communicated their (political) commons.

This commensality, however, was not limited to relations within city-states, but also covered relations between them. It was relevant, therefore, to the creation of a diplomatic community as well. The official welcoming of foreign ambassadors always involved a gastronomic practice in the form of a public luncheon.[14] Such was also the case with the welcoming back of one's own ambassadors. Athenian ambassadors were always given "an invitation to the public dinner in the Town Hall" after the end of their mission. Demosthenes, for example, points out in an oration that because this custom was not extended in the embassy of Aeschines, it must have been a sign of disapproval for his overall ambassadorial conduct: "We are told that these compliments had never before been withheld from any ambassadors since the foundation of Athens—not even from Timagoras, whom the Assembly condemned to death."[15] The significance of the ambassadors' meals (with coambassadors and also foreign ones) lay in the fact that those who shared in food and drink also shared in thought and diplomatic conduct. For instance, Demosthenes was accused of being a bad ambassador because he drank water instead of wine, something that made him awkward to negotiate with![16] In another instance, in *The Iliad*, Achilles threatened to slay Priam, the king of Troy who had gone to the Greek camp to ask for the dead body of Hector, if he did not join him for supper. Achilles maintained that after their agreement on the release and despite Priam's grief, it was only proper that they "turn their thoughts to supper."[17]

This sharing in communion among a city's ambassadors and among ambassadors of different cities was therefore responsible for establishing a diplomatic community and a primordial *corps diplomatique*. Aeschines uses precisely this argument in his own oration and submits that Demosthenes could not accuse him of misconducting the embassy to Philip because he (Demosthenes) joined the ambassadors' meal. If he sat, ate, and drank with the other Athenian ambassadors, he also joined them in thought, policy, and diplomatic conduct: "Where is the salt of friendship? where is the genial board? where is the cup of communion?"[18] Demosthenes accepts the argument but maintains that in the case of a false embassy (*parapresbeia*) what takes priority is "the salt of the city and the table of the state"; in other words, the common meal he shares with his fellow Athenians is more important and even compels him to overrule the common meal of the ambassadors of a corrupted embassy.[19]

In addition, the common meal that followed the sacrifice (*thusia*) was employed for the conclusion and ratification of a treaty. Linguistic agreement was never enough for a treaty to enter into force. Philip of Macedonia fully exploited the situation for military advantages: when the Athenian ambassadors returned with an embassy to ratify a peace treaty already agreed (to participate in the sacrifice, the common meal, and the taking of the oaths), Philip was nowhere to be found. This common meal that followed the sacrifice included the gods and served as a form of communication between the ambassadors and, more important, between them and the gods:

> The distinction between the shares allocated to men and gods in the sacrifice . . . stresses the difference that now separates them, their membership in two distinct races. Just as this former proximity was mythically expressed by the image of a community of guests enjoying a banquet together, the eventual separation is reflected in the contrast between two types of eating. The difference between diets found at the very heart of the ritual seeks, however, to establish a kind of contract and communication between the two races, a bond that leads as much as possible, to building a bridge between the earth and heaven.[20]

Furthermore, libation (*sponde*) was equally important. Libation was a drink offering and a drinking bout between the city's representatives and the gods, for wine was first poured out on the ground for the gods and subsequently shared among the ambassadors. That also signified the effective conclusion and ratification of the treaty, solemnizing the treaty and making it sacrosanct; not even the gods who participated in the drinking bout could break it.[21] The word for libation, *sponde,* was therefore also used to denote a treaty. An informal agreement or truce was known as *aspondos* (no libation or drinking bout) and so was of no legal value.[22] Thus, *ekekheiria* (truce) was literally understood as the restraining of the hand—restraining in terms of aggression but also in terms of sharing in the eats and drinks of the common meal.

In ancient Greece, therefore, participation in common meals was constitutive of political and diplomatic community. It promoted unity and solidarity in the polis, but also figured as a strategic construction in establishing a diplomatic corps that assumed collective responsibility. Furthermore, commensality was an instrument for the conclusion and ratification of a treaty, rendering it sacrosanct by way of a festive meal between the different parties and the gods. In consuming the eats and drinks of the sacrifice, the treaty itself was consummated. This final aspect of ancient Greek diplomatic practice is of particular interest as it introduces the idea of communication with the gods through communion. This type of communication with the sacred is to be later exhibited in the Christian doctrine of the Holy Communion (*theia koinonia*).

BIBLICAL FORMS OF GASTRONOMIC DIPLOMACY

Gastronomy as a way of constituting community and as a form of communication also figures in the Bible. There are numerous instances in the Old Testament where eating and drinking are employed as powerful metaphors or symbols: for example, the eating of the forbidden fruit that precipitated the Fall in the Genesis (3:1–14) or the drinking of Jeremiah's wine of wrath that caused all other nations to go mad (Jer. 25:15–16). But it is in Exodus that gastronomy attains a foundational role for the Jewish community. The Passover meal has both a religious and an ethnic significance; it symbolizes Israelite freedom from Egyptian bondage. Through it, the Israelites manage to avoid the divine mortal blow against all first-born that strikes Egypt by following the detailed culinary, eating, and protocol instructions of their master-chef deity:

> On the tenth day of this month let every man procure a lamb or kid for his family, one for every household. . . . Your lamb shall be without blemish, a male of the first year: ye shall take it from the sheep, or from the goats: and ye shall keep it up until the fourteenth day of the same month: and the whole assembly of the congregation of Israel shall kill it at even. And they shall take of the blood, and put it on the two side posts and on the lintel, upon the houses wherein they shall eat it. And they shall eat the flesh in that night, roast with fire, and unleavened bread; with bitter herbs they shall eat it. Eat not of it raw, nor sodden at all with water, but roast with fire; its head with its legs and with the inwards thereof. And ye shall let nothing of it remain until the morning; but that which remaineth of it until the morning ye shall burn with fire. And thus shall ye eat it; with your loins girded, your shoes on your feet, and your staff in your hand: and you shall eat it in haste: it is the Lord's passover. (Exod. 12:3–11)

The Passover meal separates the Israelites as the chosen community saved from foreign domination. Its commemoration is therefore not just a means of remembering and thanksgiving but also, more important, a way of constituting the Israelites as a distinct community, a community that subscribes to special gastronomic laws and excludes on dietary basis: "Throughout your generations ye shall keep it a feast by an ordinance for ever. Seven days shall ye eat unleavened bread; even the first day ye shall put away leaven out of your houses: for whoever eateth leavened bread from the first day until the seventh day, that soul shall be cut off from Israel" (12:14–15).

Furthermore, this religious gastronomy could be made available only to the foreigner who becomes a member of the community—in other words, only to the fully domesticated other: "This is the ordinance of the passover: there shall no alien eat thereof: but every man's servant that is bought for money, when thou hast circumcised him, then shall he eat thereof. . . . And when a stranger shall sojourn with thee, and will keep the passover to the Lord, let all his males be circumcised" (12:43–48). In short, the discourse of the Passover meal as narrated in the Old Testament inscribes an ethnic-religious community based on a special diet and maintained by way of gastronomic conformity.

In the New Testament, gastronomy figures again as a means of establishing community and as an even more direct way of communicating with the sacred. Christian gastronomy acquires a different theological significance. In the form of the Eucharist, it commemorates the act of sacrifice of the Son of God for the redemption of humankind. It becomes a special medium for divine communication and for the transmission of the Christian message.[23] But the Holy Communion can be also seen as a gastronomic device for creating an ecumenical community, a religious community that seeks to transcend ethnic ones (Israelite, Greek, and Roman).

The Eucharist was initiated in the Last Supper, which is another archetype of gastronomic diplomacy, of food and drink as a mediatory process, a process of communication through a banquet of remembrance, a Holy Communion (of Jesus with his disciples and of them with the sacred). As is the case with all official dinners, the Last Supper was well managed and prepared in advance; Jesus instructed Peter and John to deal with the necessary arrangements for the Passover meal celebration (Luke 22:7–13). The seating arrangement was also important. As pictured in religious paintings, it follows certain precedence: Jesus (the host) is at the center of the table and next to him his favorite apostles (Peter and John), whereas the apostate

(Judas) is usually pictured at the very end of the table, as if ready to leave. During the Last Supper, Jesus informed his disciples of the dinner's importance: "With desire I have desired to eat this passover with you before I suffer" (Luke 22:15). It is a special supper, the very last of the mundane ones: "I will not eat it, until it be fulfilled in the kingdom of god. . . . I will not drink from henceforth of the fruit of the vine, until the kingdom of god shall come" (Luke 22:16, 18). Then follows the drama of the gastronomic apotheosis: "And he took bread and when he had given thanks he brake it, and gave to them, saying, This is my body which is given for you: this do in remembrance of me. And the cup in like manner after the supper, saying, This cup is the new covenant in my blood, which is poured out for you" (Luke 22:19–20). Thus, through the consumption of the body and blood of the sacrificed deity, the Last Supper gastronomically concluded the new Christian covenant. To that extent, the First Communion serves as a gastronomic instrument by which Christians ratify the covenant, and the Eucharist, in general, as a means of continuously acknowledging their commitment to it.

In his First Letter to Corinthians, Paul codifies this gastronomic doctrine of the new Christian community. Paul recalls the Last Supper but also acknowledges the tradition of the Hebrew forefathers, who in establishing their community "did all eat the same spiritual meat; and did all drink the same spiritual drink" (1 Cor. 10:3–4). The Christians are allowed a relatively flexible and balanced diet: "[Eat] whatsoever is sold in the shambles, asking no questions for conscience sake; for the earth is the Lord's, and the fullness thereof" (10:25–26). They are instructed, nevertheless, not to join a feast where food and drink has been sacrificed to pagan deities because this unavoidably results in commensality and communion with these false gods: "But I say, that the things which the Gentiles sacrifice, they sacrifice to devils, and not to God: and I would not that ye should have communion [koinonous] with devils. Ye cannot drink the cup of the Lord, and the cup of devils: ye cannot partake of the table of the Lord, and of the table of devils" (10:20–21). Paul further dictates that only members—and worthy members—of the church can share in the sacred gastronomy associated with the body and blood of Christ; for instance, a degree of gastronomic obedience in terms of fasting needs to take place before one qualifies to receive the Holy Communion. For the Eucharist is no ordinary food and drink, and so an unworthy Christian sharing in this extraordinary communion may eat and drink oneself to damnation:

> Wherefore whosoever shall eat the bread or drink the cup of the Lord unworthily, shall be guilty of the body and the blood of the Lord. But let man prove himself, and so let him eat of the bread, and drink of the cup. For he that eateth and drinketh, eateth and drinketh judgment unto himself, if he discern not the body. (11:27–29)

The baptismal act initiates entry but in itself is never enough for continuous membership in the Christian community. By regulating access to divine gastronomy, Paul envisages a situation in which a member may be temporarily or permanently excluded from the church sacraments (that is, communion abstinence or excommunication). Such condition effectively means a breaking of communication between that member and God, itself a guarantee of eternal damnation unless communication is reestablished prior to death (if the sinner repents for his sins and receives the Last Communion).

MODERN FORMS OF GASTRONOMIC DIPLOMACY

So far, I have suggested that in ancient Greece gastronomy was a medium by which the Greeks integrated their political community, created an embryonic diplomatic corps, and communicated between different communities and their gods. I have also shown how gastronomy was foundational for the constitution of Jewish and Christian communities, and for their communication with the sacred. As I intend to suggest below, gastronomy plays its role as well for the establishment of modern diplomatic community and communication.

Modern diplomatic practice is conventionally identified with the principles and rules introduced in mid-fifteenth-century Italy, later adopted and developed in Renaissance Europe, and codified in the Treaty of Westphalia (1648) and the Congress of Vienna (1815).[24] In that period, the European diplomatic community formed, in Hedley Bull's terminology, an "international society" sharing common interests, rules, culture, and institutions.[25] Although its most important common feature was Christianity, there were also other means employed for self-consolidation (such as civilizing processes, humanism, scientific rationality). Gastronomic practices had their own role to play in fostering a distinctive European community. For example, Marco Polo's travels, which became a considerable source of knowl-

edge on the Oriental other, provide long and detailed stories of the
eating peculiarities of the Kublai Khan, drawing particularly on de-
viations from European practices. These differences were further reinforced by the rediscovery and subsequent popularity of such clas-
sics as Plinius's *Historia Naturalis*. Plinius offered depictions of
monstrous human races, which included a number of gastronomic
perversions such as the Anthropophagi (cannibals), the Polyphagi
(eaters of many peculiar species), the Panphagi (eaters of everything),
the Agriophagi (eaters of the meat of wild animals), the turtle-eaters,
the locust-eaters, the Cynamolgi (dog-milkers), the Astomi (mouth-
less who eat from other orifices). European gastronomy, and by that,
European community, differed precisely in its abstinence from such
omnivorous practices.

In *The Conquest of America*, Tzvetan Todorov shows how the
"discoverers" used, among other things, dietary differences to justify
their conquest and domination, with particular reference to "the
portentous crime of devouring human flesh."[26] Cannibalism did not
only challenge the natives' basic humanity but also their very ability
to make distinctions between right and wrong: "The consumption of
human flesh and of lower species of animals or plants (rats, snakes,
locusts, worms, roots, berries, and so on) were indications of a failure to respond to the presence of pollution and to make satisfactory
distinctions between the edible and the inedible."[27] By this rationale,
the native Americans did not represent civilized communities with
which the Europeans could partake in communion—that is, rationally articulate and exchange their political commons. Their eating
habits, especially cannibalism, reinforced the imperial perception
that these were communities of low humanity and intelligence with
which communication could only be very basic.

But gastronomy had its significance in the constitution of a diplomatic community, even in cases when there were no extreme differences in dietary practices. In such instances, habits relating to gastronomy reproduced cultural difference, which in turn was used to
justify diplomatic exclusion. The particular example here is the Ottoman Empire, with which the Europeans engaged in constant diplomatic communication, though never accepting as part of the European "international" community until the mid-nineteenth century.[28]
Although again religion was the primary reason for the exclusion of

the Ottoman Empire, gastronomical differences played their role in radicalizing the perception of Ottoman otherness. Seen from a different perspective, they also reinforced the perception of Western otherness. Apart from the obvious dietary differences (such as eating pork and drinking alcohol), there were other significant ones that left a strong impression on Mehmet Efenti, the Ottoman ambassador sent on a special mission to France in 1721 to examine European cultural practices. He therefore noted them down for information to the sultan. For the French, the meal at court was a big social event taking place in huge dining rooms. They were seated on chairs around a table mixed with women. The meal had to be eaten slowly and politely, and the guests talked to each other. This clearly shocked the Ottomans who were used to small, private meals; had no dining rooms (they were served in their living quarters); had their women eat separately; used to eat with haste and in total silence; and did not use napkins, forks, knives, plates, or salt. This gastronomic exoticism of Eastern versus Western eating habits reached its climax when the Ottoman ambassador received a peculiar—though for the French nobility not uncommon—request:

> They wanted, in particular, to watch us eat. We received messages that the daughter of so-and-so or the wife of so-and-so requested permission to watch us eat. We could not always refuse. Since [our eating times] coincided with their fast, they would not eat but surround the dining table and watch us. Since we were not accustomed to such behaviour, this distressed us very much. We endured with patience out of our consideration for them.[29]

In Renaissance Europe, gastronomic practices at court acquire high social significance and establish an order of communication mediating the relations of kings and nobility. Gastronomy now formed part of a wider social project, a "civilizing process" that refined behavior in such areas as table manners (proper use of cutlery, instruction in the combinations of food and drink, how to talk or blow one's nose while eating, and so on).[30] Diplomacy, to that extent, is not merely gastronomical, it is also gastrological. It is logic as in gastro-logic, dealing with the choice of food and wine, placement, table manners: for example, "seating people correctly is necessary to avoid 'uncertainty and confusion' and take into account 'national sensitivity.'"[31] As Contessa Giuseppina Pietromarchi reminded us in a symposium on the contemporary role of the diplomatic wife: "Lunches, cocktails, gatherings, well-appointed tables, successful dinners. These are not just small details but rather a vital point of any diplomatic mission abroad."[32] Failure to enter this logic is also failure to discharge diplomacy in its very important ceremonial and civilized mode.[33]

In this respect, a considerable amount of diplomatic time and effort is currently being spent on preparing and fully attending to the requirements of official dinners. Robert Moore calculates 900 hours spent "formally at table or at cocktail parties," which amounts to 113 working days: "Such time as [the diplomat] can spare from the adorning of dinners he may devote to the neglect of his duties."[34] Moore nonetheless congratulates the "creative co-operation between representatives of sovereign states" (in this instance, the High Commissioners and the Canada Department of External Affairs) for time well spent in producing a recipe book (43). Gastronomic diplomacy, it seems, cannot be avoided.

That is why for a diplomat to abstain from an official dinner is also to abstain from the acts of diplomatic communion and, inevitably, from the acts of diplomatic communication: "If a diplomat did try to opt out, other countries' diplomats would regard his actions as a deliberate snub. 'You entertain and you have to go to other people's functions or they will draw conclusions about you and your relations with their country.'"[35] Absence or "diplomatic illness" signifies a break or severance of relations, a state of incommutability and incommunication with the state that offers the immolation: a voluntary abstention or a more serious involuntary exclusion from the sacraments of mediation (perhaps downgraded diplomatic relations), or an even more permanent sentence of excommunication (no diplomatic relations at all).[36] So to consume the eats and drinks of an official meal is also to consume the very diplomatic act that rendered them available.

A dinner may also be a way of initiating or resisting diplomatic acts. In the case of the Himalayan kingdom of Sikkim, it was regularly employed in the 1960s and 1970s as a cherished means of diplomatic contact and ceremonial recognition, one that always reflected on the question of Sikkimese sovereignty. To gain the ear of a visiting VIP the Gangtok palace always had a buffet:

> In this way cordons of Sikkimese officers can outflank him and talk
> to him about Sikkim while another detachment pins down the Indian
> Representative and his aides so they can't intervene. If we are seated,
> the dinner is a loss, as the guest of honour is always placed next to
> me, and I'm not supposed to say anything.[37]

And, at least once, an hors d'oeuvre from the palace frustrated the
plans of the Indian representative, who in breaking with etiquette in-
vited first a group of military aides from different countries to the
India House. The palace was left with the less important cocktail
party but decided nonetheless to give them dinner on toothpick:
"Anything that has a toothpick in it counts as an *hors d'oeuvre*. That
evening the VIPs, surfeited with the battery of toothpick-stuck
courses they've been served, stagger out from our reception groaning
at the thought of the upcoming dinner."[38] It was a highly symbolic,
gastronomic resistance intended to frustrate India's host status and
annexation plans.

But at times, this gastronomic knowledge needs to be exhibited,
as wine, in particular, can form the basis of serious conversation at
dinner parties and a source of grave embarrassment and diminishing
influence for the uninitiated in the eyes of fellow diplomats. Wine
discourse, therefore, becomes of the utmost importance when it in-
terlinks with diplomatic discourse. In such cases, it is much more
than table talk. At this point, it is no longer wine but diplomacy that
is poured in the crystal glasses; it is diplomacy that excites the palatal
sense in the diplomat's mouth; and it is also diplomacy that intoxi-
cates the mind of the diplomat. Thus advice for diplomats, a guiding
note on the key words to be circulated at the table:

> I am sure you must have noticed at dinner parties, formal or informal,
> and whether you know the other guests well or just have met them,
> after the small talk about the weather, politics . . . *serious conversa-
> tion inevitably turns to wine. It is therefore important that you ex-
> press yourself in the correct terms.* If you wish to pass general
> favourable comments on the character of the wine you refer to it as
> rich, clean, elegant, full, vigorous, robust, tasty, soft or velvety. If
> your comments are not so favourable you might mention—out of
> your host's earshot of course—that the wine is poor, harsh, unbal-
> anced, heavy or thin. Raising your glass and looking at the liquid
> against the light, if you are pleased with the sight you refer to a bril-
> liant, clear, ruby or amber wine. If you don't like the contents of your

glass you mutter about it being dull, faded and cloudy. Raising the glass to your lips and tasting it for alcohol content, if you like it you might call it generous, powerful and lively. If you do not, then call it lifeless, cold, flat and weak. . . .

In judging the sugar content of wine, favourable terminology should include the words dry or sweet, mellow, silky or smooth. If you hate it label it harsh or sugary. Lifting the glass to your nose, smell the wine. If you feel good about it, talk of a fine, perfumed, fruity, and rich-in-bouquet wine; but if you don't like it mention the smell of cork and refer to "a flatness."[39]

This is consequently a medium for practicing diplomacy in its gastrological mode, of discharging one's diplomatic, official duties through vinous discourse.

TOWARD A GLOBAL POLITICS OF GASTRONOMY?

Goethe once warned that "he who cannot draw on three thousand years is living from hand to mouth." This short genealogy of gastronomy has its value in showing how from early premodern to contemporary diplomatic affairs, the eating and drinking of the commons could be seen as both a political and a politicizing process. Commensality and dietary practices figure as forms—and at times, even as an organized system—of communication and as a means of producing an imagined political-diplomatic community. Theological discourse plays its own distinctive part in this process. As shown above, the breaking of the bread, the eating of the flesh, the drinking from the cup of communion inscribe their own logics of memory and commemoration. Historical and contemporary diplomatic feasts are primarily feasts of remembrance, sacrifices to the glory of "mortal gods," and thus also commemorations of sovereignty and subjectivity.

Of course, in this chapter, I have only had space to outline some implications of gastronomic practices for our understanding of how diplomacy itself is practiced. The political effects of the gastronomic project are, however, far from being exhausted and, I believe, are in need of further exploration elsewhere. Moreover, this discussion was limited mainly to Western gastronomic practices, and to that extent its propositions beg the investigation of non-Western practices, not only to redress an imbalance but also because of the richness and differences in them (for example, the political uses of Gandhian fasting as a means of peaceful mobilization that are yet to be fully explored).[40] For that matter, the same applies to the more general understanding of gastronomy in areas like that of hunger strikes and their use as forms of resistance to national policy and injustice all over the world. Note, however, how a hunger strike may, for instance, be a way by which the powerless seek to register their political grievances but also an act of mental terrorism or an act that betrays an ethic of heroic sacrifice. The power relations and micropolitics of such acts, therefore, should be carefully examined for their effects. Yet there is another private dimension of gastronomy that cannot be ignored: the meaning of dietary practices and abstinence as ascesis for spiritual fulfillment and enlightened liberation. In this respect, the popular growth of vegetarianism is an interesting development in terms of its critique of animal exploitation, utilitarianism, and anthropocentrism but also as a way of fostering a different relation to beings and nature.

In the end, it may be that all these gastronomic diversions are nothing less than a way of practicing politics and diplomacy differently.

THEOREMA

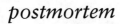

postmortem

An analysis or enquiry into an event, primarily to see what lessons can be learnt from it (Latin: "after the death").
—RALPH FELTHAM, Diplomatic Handbook

Hermes Trismegistus, from Achilles Bocchius, *Symbolicarum Quaestionum*, Bologna, 1555

The Revelation of Hermes

According to the Kore Kosmou [a Hermetic text] Hermes was a god who succeeded in understanding the mysteries of the Heavens, and revealed them by inscribing them in sacred books, which he then hid here on earth, intending that they should be searched for by future generations, but found only by the fully worthy.—GARTH FOWDEN, The Egyptian Hermes

Theoria, or "contemplation," is the word given to the experience of the eternal, as distinguished from all other attitudes, which at most may pertain to immortality. It may be that the philosophers' discovery of the eternal was helped by their very justified doubt of the chances of the polis *for immortality or even permanence.*—HANNAH ARENDT, The Human Condition

Our journey is now approaching its conclusion; the end of theoria is imminent. But not without aporias concerning its way. Was it the right way? Was it a long and unnecessary way? Was it a circular way? Was it a public, scholarly road or a private, arduous path? Does it lead to the oracle? Does it give a prophecy, a *theorema*?

It may be helpful therefore to retrace the journey so far. It seems that it passed through local, national, and global sites as well as philosophical, mythological, etymological, and artistic territories. On the way, different manifestations of theoria (*theoris, thema, theama,* and *theon-ora*) were used to shed light on diplomacy, while at the same time different manifestations of diplomacy (*démarche, ius legationis, fait accompli, coup de main, protocol,* and *hors-d'oeuvre*) threw light on practices of theory. In *démarche* diplomacy was suggested as a frame-up. Diplomatic representations were shown to be attuned to the framing of the modern world picture, that is, working under the assumption of sovereign presence while forgetting the conditions that make such presence possible. To that extent, the constantly reproduced reality of the diplomatic framework was highly problematized.

Ius legationis addressed the framed condition of diplomacy by inverting and deconstructing the way embassy has been conventionally theorized. This initiated a theoretical approach that involved doing three things: first, attempting to appropriate the Western philosophical tradition within which diplomacy is thought of in a more resourceful way, by retrieving originary understandings of both diplomacy and theory in different historical epochs; second, exposing the dissemination of meanings or multiple interpretations of messages, that is, manifesting the impossibility of foreclosing the questions of theory and diplomacy once and for all; and third, employing the very discourse of diplomatic practice for retheorizing diplomacy.

Fait accompli examined the diplomatic theory-practice problematic and its conventional application. By unsettling this distinction by means of the term *theoria,* it was argued that theory is implicated in the very practice it seeks to understand, and so it needs itself to be explained before it starts doing the explaining. It became necessary, consequently, to retrieve the early notions of *theoria*—journey, attentive look, and sacred embassy—and to work further on the contemporary implications of interlacing theory and diplomacy.

Following the problematization of the theory-practice distinction, I unsettled in the *coup de main* section the binary oppositions of word/thing, speaking/thinking, and speaking/writing. Here I investigated the duplicity of writings in crafting the theme of diplomacy as well as the sovereign practices of inscription and textual strategies of exclusion (that is, suppressing other themes of the word *diplomacy* that are not associated with statecraft). *Protocol* dealt with the philosophicopolitical association between theoria and theater and examined the *theamatic* aspect of theory and the necessary fictions for staging and performing diplomacy. *Hors d'oeuvre* engaged in a reading of diplomatic communion, specifically dealing with the production and consumption of diplomatic commons out of marginal practices like gastronomy. In other words, it showed how a political and diplomatic community is created and a form of communication established through dietary practices and acts of commensality.

Inevitably, the question will be raised of what is the use of the theoric journey, the value of such approach? So far, critical IR approaches (particularly the so-called postmodern ways) have been coldly received, when not vehemently dismissed, by those at the center of the discipline.[1] But in rejecting them IR disciplinarians most often apply standards that these new approaches have already put to question and have highly problematized (for example, fixed identity or technical concerns). At other times, they seem to cry impenetrable language, claiming that the terminology used is difficult to understand, as if a scholarly genre owes a duty of intelligibility to those who often make little or no effort to learn the language it speaks; or as if the language of the so-called realists that speaks of "national interest" and "balances of power" is perfectly intelligible to those in whose name it is practiced (for instance, was it perfectly intelligible to the current U.S. president during the Vietnam War?); or as if language is a simple exercise in correspondence and not a complex network of significations and contested meanings. Yet at other times, it is "the underlying amoralism of post-modernism, with its denial of any generally applicable moral principles,"[2] that constitutes the problem of such an approach, again, as if the application of general moral principles may not be the cause of the problem (for example, doing the "right thing" in Nazi Germany or even apparently democratic regimes),[3] or as if those who reflect on the "nothingness" of principles could not have an ethical or compassionate relationship with others (for instance, and perhaps more so, in the case of Tibetan lamas).[4] One can draw lists of one-thousand-times-heard, denouncing attributions that, despite suggestions to the opposite, have already been consistently and seriously dealt with.[5] I do not intend to address them once again here, other than to concur that there is indeed a limited application for this and other critical projects when viewed from a statecentric perspective or judged with disciplinarian expectations.

That critical approaches do not fit dominant global agendas or immediately answer framed political dilemmas can be accepted. But what cannot be accepted is that they have no empirical value or that they are apolitical. On the one hand, the discourse of technocrats or the study of governmental data should not be seen as the only empirical source in world politics. Artistic or textual sites provide spaces where politics are read differently and offer their own empirical insight or experience (*empereia*). To say that only traditional or officially defined areas of interest are empirical is to argue that only certain (sovereign) types of political representation matter. But Antonio Gramsci, Walter Benjamin, and Michel Foucault, among others, have shown how one can ignore cultural artifacts or micropolitical practices—branding them as part of aesthetics and not as sites of power—only at a great risk. It appears increasingly necessary to examine the multiple representations of politics and diplomacy (from cinema, television, and advertising to ecological and world-music movements) in a period when these representations are transmitted in ever higher speeds and massively experienced as readily available codes for deciphering the world.[6]

On the other hand, critical approaches that stubbornly endure in questioning should not be viewed as devoid of practical concern or political action. When Socrates was challenged for always asking philosophical questions instead of dealing with the serious affairs of the polis, he replied that he was "one of few Athenians, not to say the only one, who attempts the true political art [*alethos politike techne*] and practices politics [*prattein ta politika*]."[7] (This form of politicization comes from a man who still admitted that when he had been elected member of the council while his tribe held the presidency, he did not know the voting procedure.)[8] We do not need to go down Plato's road of the philosopher-ruler to accept the Socratic proposition that the one who constantly questions the grounds on which politics is conducted has an important political role, even if, and perhaps more when, the area or line of questioning appears to be outside everyday political concerns. Yet what is political and nonpolitical is one of the issues that should remain open to the possibility of such questioning. A lot is politically at stake in safeguarding the manifoldness of the political—and for that matter, the diplomatic—way.

That is why, concerning the way, the figure of Hermes could be helpful—Hermes being the god of diplomacy but also of language and travelers. And there is no one better, it seems, through which to address a postmortem, for Hermes was also the guide of souls to their final destination (*psychopompos*).[9] Hermes took charge when a mortal's journey was concluded and when the moment of truth arrived. Who then is Hermes? Or, rather, what forms and manifestations did the ancient Greeks see in Hermes (or for that matter, the Romans in Mercury, or the Egyptians in Thoth)? What do the ways of Hermes involve? First, the association of Hermes with diplomacy is significant; he is the messenger of the gods and he is the deity under whose special tutelage diplomacy is practiced. Harold Nicolson points to this mythological link even to the extent of suggesting that "the choice of this deity had an unfortunate effect upon the subsequent repute of the Diplomatic Service. . . . Later diplomatists have often regretted that someone less brilliant but more reliable was not chosen as their tutelar deity."[10] For Hermes is a polymorphous divinity of multiple and disparate characters. As mentioned, he is the god of travelers (*hodias*), the first to open roads (*hegemonios*), and the one who marks the way (herms, *hermai*, were the stones marking the direction and distance along the road). Furthermore, he guides shepherds and their flock (*kriophoros*), although he often leads them astray.[11] He protects merchants and all kinds of commerce (*nomios, epimelios*); he is the god of reciprocal exchanges (*epamoibina erga*), but he is also the god of thieves and a thief himself (stealing the herd of Apollo).[12] He is the god of hinges (*propulaios, strophaios*), guarding the integrity of doors, regulating the inside from the outside, and so ensuring access or inaccessibility from the one to the other. He is the giver of good luck but also of bad luck (*hermaion* in ancient Greek meant both). He is the god of traps and machinations, a trickster (*dolios*), a god of deceit and double-talk who even lies to Zeus, but it is precisely his rhetorical capacity that elevates him to an immortal (the only god who was born mortal but negotiated his immortality, who became an other, and the messenger of that other). Hermes is also the god of rituals who nonetheless personally violates the elementary rules of sacrifice, engaging in an insolent reversal, mixing the divine with the human portions of the sacrificed animal.[13] In the Egyptian pantheon, he is a magician, a source of divine knowledge, an alchemist and a healer but also a participator in violent conspiracies, usurpations, and generally the creator of trouble.[14] Hermes, in other words, appears as a mediator, constituting and working at the boundaries between different worlds, joining what is separate, but he is also an unsettling figure, an underminer of both divine and human order, an advance transgressor of the boundaries he sets to cross, and a subversive of the worlds he is supposed to mediate. Hermes does not simply carry metaphysical messages or divine ordinances but also engages in their radical interpretation and subversion.

Some of these Hermetic ways, as Nicolson suggests, do of course call attention to traditional attributes of diplomatic practice, that is to say, duplicity and rhetorical play. Adopting them supports the study of diplomatic theory-as-practice (for example, the postmodern play with words and meanings, and the subversion of single interpretations that is after all the common work of diplomats). But note that these ways of Hermes are also expressed philosophically in the Derridean, deconstructive approach, which transgresses sovereign boundaries, unsettles metaphysical categories, mediates estranged textual territories, and denies the possibility of fixed meanings, as the contexts within which they are constituted constantly shift. Although Derrida aims at bringing to a halt a certain type of sovereign hermeneutics, I do not think, as John Caputo suggests, that he aims "at putting Hermes out of job."[15] Hermes is a diverse and devious figure that cannot be done away with so easily. In his book *Dissemination*, Derrida acknowledges that the Egyptian Thoth, just like the Greek Hermes, "had several faces, belonged to several eras, lived in several homes," requiring that "the discordant tangle of mythological accounts in which he is caught should not be neglected."[16] Further, Derrida sees in the different functions of Thoth not a permanent identity but "the subversive dislocation of identity in general, starting with that of theological regality" (86). This divinity has special significance because according to the myth, quoted by Plato, it is Thoth, this dubious figure, who invented writing. The messenger-god figures also as the signifier-god, the medium is thus also the message, and, consequently, language appears more ingenious and subtle than the metaphysics of presence let us imagine.

Although the critique of metaphysics rejects the transcendental embassy of Egyptian Thoth or Greek Hermes, as argued in the *ius legationis* section above, there is still, perhaps, a place for this curious figure in critical IR theory. For, in the figure of Hermes, the main philosophical and political issues discussed in this book are effectively combined; this figure is at the same time a medium, a message, and an interpreter. The message he carries is already an interpretation. By virtue of his character, Hermes warns the recipients of the message that the meaning can never be authentic, prompting them not to accredit an ultimate interpretive version, or to do so at a great risk. Here Hermetic untrustworthiness has a great value, constantly reminding the recipients of what is politically at stake in accrediting embassies and adopting their word—that is to say, the danger of the revelatory dimension of the message that accredits a final truth or vocabulary and calls on recipients to act accordingly and on the basis of it. The critical task, to that extent, is never to cease looking for the Hermes of language. Hermes indicates how theoria and the study of diplomacy should remain open to the work of hermeneutics,[17] while accepting the possibility of hermetism, that is, the possibility that something always remains hidden.

In a way this is also what the *theorema* of theoria was about. Heraclitus rephrased the Delphic epigram "Know Thyself" in the following way: "The Lord whose oracle is at Delphi neither declares nor hides but gives a sign."[18] In other words, Heraclitus warned that the divine message did not absolutely reveal or hide the truth. It gave a sign that was open to multiple interpretations, a truth that was bound to be cryptic (*kryptike*), derisive (*skoptike*), and equivocal (*diphoroumeni*).[19] The divine saying did not constitute a revelatory conclusion but a new hermeneutical beginning that was referred back to the polis, that is, initiating new political debates concerning its meaning and implications.[20]

The thesis put forward in this book, therefore, is that language should not be treated as an unproblematic medium that delivers clear messages and offers explanatory revelations, but a medium that constitutes the message, and so a medium that—like any message— needs to be put constantly under philosophical, political, and ethical investigation. This late-modern theoric journey has been one such detailed reviewing and rethinking of the medium that claims to mediate the way of diplomacy and immediately carry us to it.

At the beginning of this chapter I have included an engraving from Achilles Bocchius's *Symbolicarum Quaestionum*. It pictures Hermes Trismegistus (thrice greatest). Did he ever exist? And can he be trusted? Hermes bears the winged hat but not the caduceus (the mace signifying the messenger's authority). He is no longer an official medium. But he still bears a message. The Latin saying explains that Hermes "continues to inform." He holds in one hand a candlestick, which sheds light and illuminates the way. This candlestick is, however, the seven-branched one of the Apocalypse. Hermes holds "the end" in his hand. With the other, he puts his finger to his lips to enjoin silence. What does Hermes reveal? The Greek inscription reads: "You have spoken a lot, only to realize that you never commanded silence."

credentials

An ambassador or minister is, on being appointed to a post, provided with Credentials, or Letters of Credence, signed by his sovereign or head of his State. Until he has formally "presented his letters" he is not formally recognized.—SIR HAROLD NICOLSON, Diplomacy

Notes

PREAMBLE

1. André Brink, *The Ambassador* (London: Flamingo, 1986), author's note, 10.

2. World Economic Forum, Davos, February 4, 1992.

3. Quoted from his speech on Independence Day, Philadelphia, July 4, 1994.

4. For theorization as voyeurism, see Edward Said, "Traveling Theory," *Raritan* 1, no. 3 (1984):41–67. Although I also adopt the notion of traveling theory, I find Said's teleological understanding problematic, particularly in the way it delimits a privileged role for theory, enveloped in emancipatory discourse.

DÉMARCHE: **Diplomatic Representations . . . or Who Framed the Ambassadors?**

1. Jacques Derrida, *Margins of Philosophy* (Sussex: Harvester Press, 1982), 313.

2. Michel Foucault, *Power/Knowledge*, ed. by Colin Gordon (London: Harvester Wheatsheaf, 1980), 122.

3. This should not, however, downgrade the fact that historically this dignified aspect of painting had a very important role to play in the practice of diplomacy and life in court. See, for example, Louis Marin, *Portrait of the King* (London: Macmillan, 1988); Roy Strong, *Art and Power* (Suffolk: Boydell Press, 1984); Jonathan Shepard and Simon Franklin, *Byzantine Diplomacy* (Belfast: Variorum, 1992), the "Art in Diplomacy" section. For Hol-

bein's role, see Jane Roberts, *Holbein and the Court of Henry VII* (Edinburgh: National Galleries of Scotland, 1993).

4. This is Heidegger's term for describing the unity of structure in representation, the "standing-together" of things in the world (physical and historical). I explain this term in detail in the second part.

5. On this point I follow the Heideggerian thesis that in the modern age thinking follows the pattern of viewing the "world picture." Foucault has used the Heideggerian thesis in his reading of Velázquez's painting, *Las Meninas*, where he notes that an examination of the painting could open up the space for the study of the very function of representation, of the representation of classical representation: "And, indeed, representation undertakes to represent itself here in all its elements, with its images, the eyes to which it is offered, the faces it makes visible, the gestures that call it into being." Michel Foucault, *The Order of Things* (London: Tavistock, 1970), 16.

6. Jean-François Lyotard, *The Postmodern Explained to Children* (London: Turnaround, 1992), 20.

7. Peter Barber, *Diplomacy: The World of the Honest Spy* (London: British Library, 1979), 60; emphasis added.

8. Ibid., 60–61.

9. James Der Derian, *On Diplomacy: A Genealogy of Western Estrangement* (Oxford: Blackwell, 1987). In a sense this points directly to the question of the frame: are the painting and comments part of Der Derian's *ergon* (main text) or are they a *parergon* (supplementary to the text for the purposes of publication)?

10. Christopher Hill's review in *International Affairs* 64, no. 1 (1987–88): 104.

11. John Carroll, *Humanism: The Wreck of Western Culture* (London: Fontana Press, 1993), 29, 32; emphasis added.

12. Linda Frey and Marsha Frey, "Fatal Diplomacy, 1541," *History Today* 40 (August 1990): 10–15.

13. See Plato, *The Republic*, Book X.

14. No preparatory drawings survive the painting, and there is no information on how the work was commissioned. It was by employing another portrait painting by Jean Clouet (1533) that Ambassador de Dinteville was "identified" in this painting. See Helen Langdon, *Holbein* (London: Phaidon Press, 1993), 64.

15. For a good summary of all the different claims, see Mary F. S. Hervey, *Holbein's "Ambassadors": An Historical Study* (London: George Bell, 1900), 5–9.

16. Ibid., 10.

17. Ibid., 11–12. This, of course, prompts additional questions: Was Holbein the Dutch painter? Was Holbein Dutch enough? Was Holbein Dutch at all? He was born in Augsburg, Southern Germany, in 1497 or

1498. In fact, *The National Gallery Collection* classifies him under German, not Dutch, art. I suppose a way out for the National Gallery concerning the nationality issue is to argue that the painting is not Holbein's but signed later in his name. This supposition will be in accordance with Le Brun's position, namely, that the painting had no signature when it was under his possession. Nonetheless, the National Gallery wishes to maintain both the ambassadorial and the Holbein link.

18. William F. Dickes, *"The Ambassadors": A Contribution to History* (London: Cassell, 1903).

19. Ibid., preface.

20. Dickes first proposed so in two articles (1896, 1901). In his book he also argued that an exhausting reading of the various astronomical instruments as set and arranged in the picture itself provides evidence of the accurate birth dates (exact year, month, day, and even hour of birth) of the two German counts palatine: Otto Henry born on April 10, 1502, at 10:33 P.M., and Philip on November 12, 1503, at 5 A.M. As to other evidence supporting the idea of a portrait of the French ambassadors, he provides counterevidence that the parchment slip was never part of the frame but a seventeenth-century fabrication.

21. Michael Levey, ed., *The National Gallery Collection* (London: National Gallery Publications, 1987), 126.

22. Indeed, the *Micro Gallery* entry notes that "the picture is in a tradition showing learned men with books and instruments." See the *Micro Gallery*, "Holbein entry," the National Gallery, London.

23. Langdon, *Holbein*, 62.

24. Levey, *The National Gallery Collection*, 126.

25. Langdon, *Holbein*, 62.

26. *Micro Gallery*, "Holbein entry."

27. Ibid.

28. Langdon, *Holbein*, 62.

29. On this point, see the *Micro Gallery* entry.

30. Carroll, *Humanism*, 32.

31. *Micro Gallery*, "Holbein entry."

32. Levey, *The National Gallery Collection*, 126.

33. The *Micro Gallery* notes that "the lute was the chief courtly instrument at the time." But Dickes has an interesting thesis that the lute is an allegory for a treaty, the lute being Alciati's emblem for *foedera* (treaty). On this point, see Hervey, *Holbein's "Ambassadors,"* 227–30.

34. *Micro Gallery*, "Holbein entry."

35. Langdon, *Holbein*, 62.

36. Ibid.

37. Ibid., 64.

38. Carroll, *Humanism*, 31.

39. Langdon, *Holbein*, 62.

40. Ibid.

41. Carroll, *Humanism*, 35.

42. Ibid., 31.

43. Jacques Derrida, *The Truth in Painting* (Chicago: University of Chicago Press, 1987), 42–43.

44. Ibid., 292.

45. William E. Connolly, *Political Theory and Modernity* (Oxford: Blackwell, 1988), 4.

46. Martin Heidegger, "The Age of the World Picture," in *The Question Concerning Technology and Other Essays* (New York: Harper & Row, 1977), 115–54.

47. Heidegger uses the verb *stellen* (to place or set) in order to associate enframing (*gestell*) with notions of representation (*vorstellen*), presence or exhibition (*darstellen*), ordering (*bestellen*), entrapping (*nachstellen*), production (*herstellen*), and disguise (*verstellen*).

48. "Enframing is the gathering together that belongs to that setting-upon which sets upon man and puts him in position to reveal the real." Heidegger, "The Question Concerning Technology," in *The Question Concerning Technology and Other Essays*, 24.

49. Martin Heidegger, "The Turning," in *The Question Concerning Technology and Other Essays*, 36.

50. Martin Heidegger, *Identity and Difference* (New York: Harper & Row, 1969), 35–36.

51. In effect, Heidegger reverses the position that understanding is a matter of getting a better picture or a clearer view of beings. This has been the case with and since Platonic speleology (where, in Book VII of *The Republic*, the task of the philosopher is pictured as an ascent out of the cave of ignorance so as to get a truer view of beings, *theoria*, and their form, *eidos*) down to Nietzschean meditations: "To understand the picture one must divine the painter. . . . Nowadays, however, the whole guild of the sciences is occupied in understanding the canvas and the paint but not the picture; one can say, indeed, that only he who has a clear view of the picture of life and existence as a whole can employ the individual sciences without harm to himself, for without such a regulatory total picture they are threads that nowhere come to an end and only render our life more confused and labyrinthine." Friedrich Nietzsche, *Untimely Meditations* (Cambridge: Cambridge University Press, 1983), 141.

52. Jacques Lacan, *The Four Fundamental Concepts of Psycho-Analysis* (London: Penguin, 1979), 89.

53. This, of course, has been vividly illustrated in the case of the Holbein painting.

54. On drawing and blindness, see Jacques Derrida, *Memoirs of the Blind: The Self-Portrait and Other Ruins* (Chicago: University of Chicago Press, 1993).

55. Foucault, *The Order of Things*, 9; emphasis added.

56. Michel Foucault, *This Is Not a Pipe* (Berkeley and Los Angeles: University of California Press, 1982), 9.

57. On circular logic and the work of art, see Heidegger, "The Origin of the Work of Art," in *Basic Writings,* ed. David F. Krell (San Francisco: HarperCollins, 1977), 149–87.

58. The way diplomats are trained and initiated into this world is well illustrated in Robert D. Schulzinger, *The Making of the Diplomatic Mind: The Training, Outlook and Style of United States Foreign Policy Officials, 1908–1931* (Middletown, Conn.: Wesleyan University Press, 1975).

59. For the impact of Italian diplomatic practices in the fifteenth century on the framework of modern diplomacy, see Matthew S. Anderson, *The Rise of Modern Diplomacy, 1450–1919* (London: Longman, 1993) and Garrett Mattingly, *Renaissance Diplomacy* (Boston: Houghton Mifflin, 1955).

It is important to note the view at the time, namely, that lenses distorted reality. It was not until the second half of the sixteenth century that lenses were accepted as useful for correcting visual deficiencies. The reason given by the duke to his ambassador for his order of eyeglasses was the need to please members of his resident court who had been asking him about this new ornament. After the first posting there was a regular dispatch of spectacles for the fashionable use of the Milanese court (some of them were for "normal vision"!) and presumably through which the court could properly then view the duke's full diplomatic splendor. See Vincent Illardi, *Studies in Italian Renaissance Diplomatic History* (London: Variorum Reprints, 1986), chap. 11.

60. François Truffaut has already touched on this point when he described the post-1918 diplomats as "professional observers," in his film, *Jules et Jim* (1962).

61. See Barry Buzan, Charles Jones, and Richard Little, *The Logic of Anarchy: From Neorealism to Structural Realism* (New York: Columbia University Press, 1993), section 3.

62. Robert O. Keohane and Joseph S. Nye, *Power and Interdependence: World Politics in Transition* (Boston: Little, Brown, 1977), vii.

63. See Mark Hoffman, "Critical Theory and the Inter-Paradigm Debate," *Millennium* 16, no. 2 (1987): 231–49.

64. See Andrew Linklater, "The Question of the Next Stage in International Relations Theory: A Critical-Theoretical Point of View," *Millennium* 21, no. 1 (1992): 77–98.

65. I refer here to the works of Richard Ashley, David Campbell, James

Der Derian, Michael Dillon, Jean Elshtain, Jim George, Bradley Klein, Michael Shapiro, R. B. J. Walker, and Cynthia Weber, among others. For the purposes of classification they have come to be identified as post-modernists/poststructuralists—and they are partly to blame for it, as they have been associated with a fashionable movement that, though cutting across intellectual disciplines, sometimes engages in its own exclusionary practices and arbitrary distinctions (the modern-postmodern one to start with). Some of their works include James Der Derian and Michael Shapiro, eds., *International/Intertextual Relations: Postmodern Readings in World Politics* (Lexington, Mass.: Lexington Books, 1989); David Campbell, *Writing Security: United States Foreign Policy and the Politics of Identity* (Manchester: Manchester University Press, 1992); David Campbell and Michael Dillon, eds., *The Political Subject of Violence* (Manchester: Manchester University Press, 1993); R. B. J. Walker, *Inside/Outside: International Relations as Political Theory* (Cambridge: Cambridge University Press, 1993); Jim George, *Discourses of Global Politics* (London: Macmillan, 1994); Cynthia Weber, *Simulating Sovereignty* (Cambridge: Cambridge University Press, 1995).

66. See Richard K. Ashley and R. B. J. Walker, "Speaking the Language of Exile: Dissident Thought in International Studies," *International Studies Quarterly* 34, no. 3 (1990): 259–68.

67. See, for example, Jim George and David Campbell, "Patterns of Dissent and the Celebration of Difference: Critical Social Theory and International Relations," *International Studies Quarterly* 34, no. 3 (1990): 269–93.

68. James Der Derian, *Antidiplomacy: Spies, Terror, Speed and War* (Oxford: Blackwell, 1992). For more on Der Derian's work, see my "Late Modern Diplomacies," *Millennium* 22, no. 1 (1993): 89–96.

IUS LEGATIONIS: The Embassy of Theory

1. See Henry Kissinger's new book, *Diplomacy* (New York: Simon & Schuster, 1994), which is basically a rerun of his White House memoirs plus an exclusively personal contact with the minds of great statesmen during the so-called great events of diplomatic history: "That is why examining how statesmen have dealt with the problem of world order—what worked or failed and why—is not the end of understanding contemporary diplomacy, though it may be its beginning" (28). For commentary on the reviews of Kissinger's book, see James Der Derian, "Great Men, Monumental History, and Not-So-Grand Theory: A Meta-Review of Henry Kissinger's *Diplomacy*," *Mershon International Studies Review* 39, no. 1 (1995): 173–80.

2. For a good historical account of these events, see Michael J. Moser

and Yeone Moser, *Foreigners within the Gates: The Legations at Peking* (Oxford: Oxford University Press, 1993).

3. Martin Heidegger, *Nietzsche: The Will to Power as Art,* vol. 1 (San Francisco: HarperCollins, 1991), 165.

4. Ibid., 152.

5. Hubert L. Dreyfus, *Being-in-the-World: A Commentary on Heidegger's Being and Time* (Cambridge, Mass.: MIT Press, 1991), 1.

6. Martin Heidegger, *On Time and Being* (New York: Harper & Row, 1972), 8–9; emphasis added.

7. See John D. Caputo, "Hermes and the Dispatches from Being," in *Radical Hermeneutics: Repetition, Deconstruction, and the Hermeneutic Project* (Bloomington: Indiana University Press, 1987), 160.

8. Martin Heidegger, *On the Way to Language* (New York: Harper & Row, 1971), 29.

9. Heidegger, *On Time and Being,* 9.

10. Martin Heidegger, "The Question Concerning Technology," 3.

11. Jacques Derrida, "Sending: On Representation," *Social Research* 49 (Summer 1982): 295.

12. Jacques Derrida, "*Envois,*" in *The Post Card: From Socrates to Freud and Beyond* (Chicago: University of Chicago Press, 1987), 64.

13. Caputo, *Radical Hermeneutics,* 167.

14. Derrida, "*Envois,*" 66.

15. Caputo, *Radical Hermeneutics,* 153.

16. Derrida, "*Envois,*" 195.

17. Jacques Derrida, "Of an Apocalyptic Tone Recently Adopted in Philosophy," *Semeia* 23 (1982): 84.

18. Derrida, "Of an Apocalyptic Tone," 89.

19. Jean Baudrillard, *The Ecstasy of Communication* (New York: Semiotext[e], 1988), 97–98.

20. Ibid., 99.

FAIT ACCOMPLI: The Quest and the Question of Diplomacy

1. The Holy See officially lost all its territories following the fall of Rome to the troops of General Cadorna on September 20, 1870, and the subsequent unification of Italy. It did not acquire any territory until the signing and ratification exchanges of the Lateran Treaty (February 11 and June 7, 1929, respectively) where Italy ceded to the Holy See the tiny Vatican city (as incorporated in special supplements of the *Acta Apostolicae Sedis*).

2. For a good summary on the process of tying diplomacy to a "legal superior" and subsequently the territorial state, see J. L. Holzgrefe, "The Ori-

gins of Modern International Relations Theory," *Review of International Studies* 15, no. 1 (1989): 11–26.

3. Another exception is the Sovereign Hospitaller Order of St. John, otherwise known as the Knights of Malta, which currently enjoys diplomatic relations with more than fifty states. See C. D'Olivier-Farran, "The Sovereign Order of Malta in International Law," *International and Comparative Law Quarterly* 3 (April 1954): 217–34; and Fra Cyril Toumanoff, "The Sovereign Order of Malta: Its nature and Its problems," an expanded discourse given at the Annual Dinner of the British Association of the Sovereign Order, November 18, 1986. Twentieth-century international organizations constitute new additions to official diplomatic contact, though strictly speaking they do not enjoy the right of active and passive legation (i.e., their "diplomatic relations" do not come under the 1961 Vienna Convention on Diplomatic Relations but are governed by other international agreements).

4. Quoted in Robert A. Graham, *The Rise of the Double Diplomatic Corps in Rome: A Study in International Practice (1870–1875)* (The Hague: Nijhoff, 1952), 3; emphasis added.

5. Ibid., 3.

6. For the value of such an approach, see Michael Shapiro, ed., *Language and Politics* (Oxford: Blackwell, 1984).

7. James E. Dougherty and Robert L. Pfaltzgraff, *Contending Theories of International Relations: A Comprehensive Survey* (New York: Harper & Row, 1981), 16–17; emphasis added.

8. Quincy Wright, "The Development of a General Theory of International Relations," in Horace V. Harrison, ed., *The Role of Theory in International Relations* (Princeton, N.J.: Van Nostrand, 1964), 17.

9. Martin Wight, "Why Is There No International Theory?," in Herbert Butterfield and Martin Wight, eds., *Diplomatic Investigations: Essays in the Theory of International Politics* (London: Allen & Unwin, 1966), 17–34.

10. Cited in Harrison, ed., *The Role of Theory in International Relations*, 3–4.

11. Wight, "Why Is There No International Theory?," 26.

12. Hedley Bull, *The Anarchical Society: A Study of Order in World Politics* (London: Macmillan, 1977), 170.

13. Harold Nicolson, *Diplomacy* (Oxford: Oxford University Press, 1963; reissued by the Institute for the Study of Diplomacy, 1988), 16.

14. Der Derian, "Mediating Estrangement: A Theory for Diplomacy," *Review of International Studies* 13, no. 2 (1987): 91.

15. See my "Late Modern Diplomacies," 90–91.

16. Der Derian, *Antidiplomacy*, 27–28.

17. Martin Heidegger, *An Introduction to Metaphysics* (New Haven, Conn.: Yale University Press, 1959), 13.

18. I use the second edition (Oxford: Clarendon Press, 1989).

19. Although tempted to use the Greek alphabet when quoting from ancient Greek texts or referring to Greek terms, I have opted for Latinization because it provides, for the non-Greek reader, a better illustration of the grammatological similarities between Greek and English terms, similarities that would otherwise not be apparent.

20. On the critical value of approaching theory-as-practice, see George, *Discourses of Global Politics*, chap. 1.

21. Martin Heidegger, "Science and Reflection," in *The Question Concerning Technology and Other Essays*, 164.

22. Luke 13:48. See further the comparison of the term in James H. Moulton and George Milligan, *The Vocabulary of the Greek Testament: Illustrated from the Papyri and Other Non-Literary Sources* (London: Hodder & Stoughton, 1929), 290.

23. Homer, *The Iliad* 7:507; 10:437 and *The Odyssey* 12:407.

24. Herodotus, *Histories*, 1:29, 30.

25. Pollux, 2.55; quoted in Henry G. Liddell and Robert Scott, *The Greek-English Lexicon* (Oxford: Clarendon Press, 1882).

26. For this point, see Sophocles, *Oedipus Tyrannos*, 1491.

27. As used by Eustathius; see Liddell and Scott, *Greek-English Lexicon*.

28. Diodorus, 14:60; quoted in Liddell and Scott, *Greek-English Lexicon*.

29. Plutarch, 2:722 B; quoted in Liddell and Scott, *Greek-English Lexicon*.

30. Ibid., 876 C.

31. Diogenes Laertius, 10:47; quoted in Liddell and Scott, *Greek-English Lexicon*.

32. Plato, *Laws*, 815 B.

33. Demosthenes, *Against Meidias*, 115.

34. Thucydides, *History of the Peloponnesian War*, 6:18.

35. Demosthenes, *Against Meidias*, 53.

36. For a detailed analysis of the functions of theoria see F. Poland, *De Legationibus Graecorum Publicis* (Leipzig, 1885), and P. Boesch, *Theoros* (Berlin: 1905).

37. The most famous theorias were those sent to the island of Delos in honor of the twin deities of Apollo and Artemis (annually for the small and every five years for the great Delias). During the period of this theoria, the city had to remain pure, which included a compulsory fasting of all citizens and prohibition of any public execution (the execution of Socrates was suspended until the return of the Delian theoria; see Plato, *Phaedo*, 58 C). Theorias to Delos were dispatched from all city-states, but the head of the theoric procession was always an Athenian. The sacred boat that carried the

delegates to Delos was called *theoris* (the same word used for path; see Herodotus, *Histories*, 6:87). The whole theoric journey was treated with solemnity from the very beginning (for example, from Piraeus in the case of Athens) but reached its highest magnificence at the arrival and the procession to the temple. This included music and dancing from the Delian virgins as well as games, sacrifices, and other festivities. In the temple the *theoroi* offered the respects of their city and consulted the oracle. The Delian theoria ended with an amphictyonic council (an early type of conference diplomacy). On their return, the Athenian *theoroi* were welcomed in Piraeus, and the Athenian citizens symbolically decorated and left open the doors of their houses.

38. Derrida illustrated how this is the case with Platonic *pharmakon* (meaning both poison and cure). See Jacques Derrida, "Plato's Pharmacy," in *Dissemination* (London: Athlone Press, 1981), 61–171.

39. Plato, *Phaedo*, 58 B.

40. Plato, *The Republic*, 556 C.

41. Plato, *Crito*, 52 B.

42. Plato, *Laws*, 720 B.

43. Ibid., 640 C.

44. Plato, *The Republic*, 517 D.

45. See, for example, Plato, *Laws*, 951 C.

46. See D. F. Astius, *Lexicon Platonicum sive vocum Platonicarum* (Berlin: Hermann Barsdorf, 1908), 67.

47. Aristotle, *Nicomachean Ethics*, 1177b, 31–32.

48. Indeed, all great lawgivers, like Lykourgos and Solon, traveled abroad to learn about other political customs but also to test their ideas. On the impact of such journeys and the borrowings of Greek philosophy, see Martin Bernal, *Black Athena: The Afroasiatic Roots of Classical Civilization* (London: Vintage, 1991).

49. See Plato, *Phaedo*, 68 B-C; Nicholas Lobkowicz, *Theory and Practice: History of a Concept from Aristotle to Marx* (Notre Dame, Ind.: Notre Dame University Press, 1967), 4; Lobkowicz offers in addition an excellent historical analysis of their use.

50. Hans Morgenthau, "Reflections on the State of Political Science," *Review of Politics* 17 (October 1955): 440.

51. As argued by Cicero and Jamblichus (who base their thesis on a lost treatise of Heracleides of Pontus), the distinction of the three lives and the prominence of the theoretical life can be traced back to Pythagoras. On dealing with the philosopher, Pythagoras allegedly offered the simile of men attending a theoria (festival, games) and so differentiated in terms of traders, participants and competitors, and spectators. The philosopher belonged to the third group (spectators) and so to theoretical life as tied to the view/

contemplation of beautiful things (*ton kalliston theorian*). See Lobkowicz, *Theory and Practice*, 5.

52. Aristotle, *Nicomachean Ethics*, 1095b, 15–18.

53. Ibid., 1095a, 6–7.

54. Aristotle, *Politics*, 1324a, 16–17.

55. Aristotle, *Nicomachean Ethics*, 1117a, 13–18.

56. *Metaphysics*, 993a, 30–993b, 12.

57. Ibid., 932b, 8.

58. Such is the case of Theophrastus who succeeded Aristotle in the presidency of the Academy and established peripatetic philosophy.

59. See Lobkowicz, *Theory and Practice*, 55.

60. Lobkowicz, *Theory and Practice*, 64.

61. Ibid., 69.

62. Martin Heidegger, "Letter on Humanism," in *Basic Writings*, 194.

63. On this point, see Hans-Georg Gadamer, "The Beginning and the End of Philosophy," in Christopher Macann, ed., *Martin Heidegger: Critical Assignments* (London: Routledge, 1992), chap. 1.

COUP DE MAIN: Diplo-ma-cy: From Statecraft to Handicraft

1. Terence A. M. Bishop, *Scriptores Regis* (Oxford: Clarendon Press, 1960), 1.

2. On such specialized uses of the hand for diplomatic signaling, see Raymond Cohen, *Theatre of Power: The Art of Diplomatic Signalling* (London: Longman, 1987), 91–102.

3. Nicolson, *Diplomacy*, 113.

4. See D. P. Heatley, *Diplomacy and the Study of International Relations* (Oxford: Clarendon Press, 1919), 11.

5. José Calvet De Magalhães, *The Pure Concept of Diplomacy* (New York: Greenwood Press, 1988), 59–60.

6. Nicolson, *Diplomacy*, 3–4.

7. R. B. Mowat, *Diplomacy and Peace* (London: Williams & Norgate, 1935), 22.

8. Eugène Scribe, *Le diplomate* (1827), quoted in William J. Roosen, *The Age of Louis the XIV: The Rise of Modern Diplomacy* (Cambridge: Schenkman, 1976), 1.

9. Carl von Clausewitz, *On War* (Princeton, N.J.: Princeton University Press, 1976), chap. 1, sect. 24.

10. Thomas Schelling, *Arms and Influence* (New Haven: Yale University Press, 1966), chap. 1.

11. See, for example, Alexander L. George and William E. Simmons, eds., *The Limits of Coercive Diplomacy* (Boulder, Colo.: Westview Press,

1994); James Cable, *Gunboat Diplomacy 1919–1991* (London: Macmillan, 1994); and Gordon A. Craig and Alexander L. George, *Force and Statecraft: Diplomatic Problems of Our Time* (Oxford: Oxford University Press, 1983), chap. 4.

12. Quoted in Der Derian, *Antidiplomacy*, 1.

13. Martin Heidegger, *What is Called Thinking?* (New York: Harper & Row, 1968), 16–17.

14. Martin Heidegger, *Parmenides* (Bloomington: Indiana University Press, 1992), 80.

15. See Jacques Derrida, "*Geschlecht* II: Heidegger's Hand," in John Sallis, ed., *Deconstruction and Philosophy: The Texts of Jacques Derrida* (Chicago: University of Chicago Press, 1987), 179.

16. See "Writing before the Letter," in *Of Grammatology* (Baltimore: Johns Hopkins University Press, 1976).

17. Martin Heidegger, *Being and Time* (Oxford: Blackwell, 1962), 95–102.

18. Dreyfus, *Being-in-the-World*, 82–83.

19. Heidegger, *On the Way to Language*, 108.

20. The politicization of themes is not unprecedented: *themata* were also the subdued provinces to which the Byzantine empire was divided.

21. Gore-Booth, ed., *Satow's Guide to Diplomatic Practice,* chap. 1, sect. 3.

22. See, for example, the 1926 edition of *Encyclopedia Britannica.*

23. See Ragnar Numelin, *The Beginnings of Diplomacy: A Sociological Study of Intertribal and International Relations* (London: Oxford University Press, 1950), 125, where he argues that *diplomacy* derives from the Greek noun, not the verb.

24. Stephen Gaselee, *The Language of Diplomacy* (Cambridge: Bowes & Bowes, 1939), 11.

25. Ibid.

26. Nicolson, *Diplomacy*, 11.

27. Ibid.

28. See Richard A. Schmutz, "The Foundation of Medieval Papal Representation" (Ph.D. diss., University of Southern California, 1966), 3–4.

29. Quoted in Gaselee, *The Language of Diplomacy*, 12.

30. Ibid., 12.

31. Ibid.

32. See Bernhard Bischoff, *Latin Palaeography: Antiquity and the Middle Ages* (Cambridge: Cambridge University Press, 1990), 1–3.

33. Ibid., 1.

34. Alexander Ostrower, *Language, Law and Diplomacy* (Philadelphia: University of Pennsylvania Press, 1965), 108–9.

35. Von Troil, *Letters on Iceland* (1780); quoted in the *OED*.

36. "History of Europe" in the *Annual Register* (1780); quoted in the *OED*.

37. "History of Europe" in the *Annual Register* (1789); quoted in the *OED*.

38. Edmund Burke, *Second Letter on a Regicide Peace*, vol. 9 of *The Collected Works of Edmund Burke* (Oxford: Clarendon Press, 1991), 282.

39. Gaselee, *The Language of Diplomacy,* 12.

40. Nicolson, *Diplomacy*, 11.

41. Note the root *diplo-*, Greek for double, the verb *diploo*, to double, the Greek root *dis-* and later Latin *duo-*, meaning two; in current English it is used also in the prefixes di(s)- and du-. Furthermore, as said above, in diploma one can see a document folded double, a diptych, and a diphyllous.

42. On the *missi* system, see Der Derian, *On Diplomacy*, 71–80.

43. W. Baldwin, ed., *A Myrroure of Magistrates* (1559); quoted in the *OED*.

44. Ruth D. Edwards, *True Brits: Inside the Foreign Office* (London: BBC Books, 1994), 169.

45. Burke, *Second Letter on the Regicide Peace*, 282.

46. Where, then, is the first, the original of this double, to be found? One can search the historical texts in vain and still not find a word *diplomacy* (in its Anglicized form) that comes prior to this one. Perhaps it was already there in the spoken discourse, having a phonetic presence that Burke copied, duplicated, and re-presented in this writing. Whatever the case, it makes no difference to our study. The point is that Burke still had to engage in an act of duplication of his own, which involved its own duplicity, in order to render diplomacy available in his text. In order to write *diplomacy,* Burke had to duplicate the written or the spoken signifier that was elsewhere, outside of his own text. Or inversely, if he is really to be held responsible for inventing a new word, Burke still had to make a double out of the thing of diplomacy—a thing or concept that was not known by this particular name before, but was copied, given a name, baptized, and became known as such thereafter. And, of course, it was redoubled again so as to describe the "double diplomacy" of Louis XV in his text. Whatever the case, Burke had to duplicate whatever he wanted to mean or name with the word *diplomacy,* as we always have to make double whenever we speak, by repeating and imitating the signs of language through which beings mean.

47. Burke, *Second Letter on a Regicide Peace*, 281–82.

48. Ibid., 281.

49. David J. Hill, *A History of Diplomacy in the International Development of Europe*, vol. 3 (London: Longman, 1914), 502.

50. George P. Gooch, *Louis XV: The Monarchy in Decline* (London: Longman, 1956), 208; emphasis added.

51. Chevalier d'Eon was a rather peculiar figure who paid full compliments to the king's double diplomacy. When again sent to London on a secret mission by Louis XV, he proved to be of dubious sexuality. At the English court he was discussed as being either a female or a hermaphrodite, rumors that "gained credibility from his feminine voice and the absence of amorous escapables." The French ambassador even dealt with the matter in his reports to Versailles: "This fiery person, so celebrated for his adventures, is a woman in man's clothes." Although a well "noted duelist," he "spent his last twenty years in female attire." Scholars are still perplexed by his significance in the diplomatic practices of the period: "The origin and purpose of his strange mystification has never been satisfactorily explained." See Gooch, *Louis XV*, 216.

52. Gooch, *Louis XV*, 209; emphasis added.

53. Ibid.

54. Burke, *Second Letter on a Regicide Peace*, 277.

55. Edmund Burke, *Thoughts on French Affairs*, vol. 8 of *The Complete Works*, 372.

56. That is how Harold Nicolson approaches it in *The Evolution of Diplomatic Method* (London: Cassell, 1954), 31.

57. R. Bernasconi, "Seeing Double," in Diane P. Michelfelder and Richard E. Palmer, eds., *Dialogue and Deconstruction: The Gadamer-Derrida Encounter* (New York: New York State University Press, 1989), 247. See further how this double reading is used to deconstruct the state in Richard K. Ashley, "Untying the Sovereign State: A Double Reading of the Anarchy Problematique," *Millennium: Journal of International Studies* 17, no. 2 (Summer 1988): 227–62.

58. Jacques Lacan, *Écrits* (London: Routledge, 1977), 43.

59. Heidegger, *Parmenides*, 148.

PROTOCOL: Diplomacy, Theater, and the Other

1. Joan Quigley, *"What Does Joan Say?" My Seven Years as White House Astrologer to Nancy and Ronald Reagan* (New York: Carol Publishing Group, 1990), 172–82.

2. R. S. Sharma, "Indian Civilization," in Harold O. Lawsswell, Daniel Lerner, and Hans Speier, eds., *Propaganda and Communication in World History: The Symbolic Instrument in Early Times*, vol. 1 (Honolulu: University of Hawaii Press, 1979), 197–98.

3. Thucydides, *History of the Pelopponesian War*, 7:50.

4. James N. Rosenau, *Global Voices: Dialogues in International Relations* (Boulder, Colo.: Westview Press, 1993), xv.

5. Roy Strong, *Art and Power: Renaissance Festivals 1450–1650* (Essex: Boydell, 1984); reprint of 1973 edition, *Splendour at Court: Renaissance Spectacle and the Theatre of Power.*

6. Cohen, *Theatre of Power*, 2.

7. Plato, *Theaetetus*, 155 D.

8. See Hesiodus, *Theogony*, 780.

9. Aristotle, *Metaphysics*, 982b, 12–14.

10. Aristotle, *Politics*, 1341a, 23.

11. Aristotle, *Poetics*, 1455a, 14.

12. Ibid., 1451a.

13. J. Peter Euben, *The Tragedy of Political Theory: The Road Not Taken* (Princeton, N.J.: Princeton University Press, 1990), 56.

14. See, for example, Baz Kershaw, *Politics of Performance: Radical Theatre as Cultural Intervention* (London: Routledge, 1992).

15. See, for example, Antonin Artaud, *Theatre and Its Double* (London: Calder, 1970); Augusto Boal, *Theatre of the Oppressed* (London: Pluto, 1979); and Richard Schechner, *Performance Theory* (New York: Routledge, 1988).

16. A detailed analysis of the *theorikon* is provided in Andreas M. Andreades, *A History of Greek Public Finance* (Cambridge, Mass.: Harvard University Press, 1933), 71, 259–63.

17. Ibid., 231.

18. Oscar G. Brockett, *History of the Theatre* (Boston: Allyn & Bacon, 1982), 25.

19. Ibid., 34.

20. Nicolson, *The Evolution of Diplomatic Method*, 26.

21. Vladimir P. Potemkin, *The History of Diplomacy*, vol. 3 (Athens: Govosti, 1974).

22. Diana Devlin, *Mask and Scene: An Introduction to a World View of Theatre* (London: Macmillan, 1989), 47.

23. See Strong, *Art and Power: Renaissance Festivals 1450–1650.*

24. In 1768, for example, the arrogant attempt by the French ambassador in London to alter the protocol arrangements that seated together the Austrian and Russian ambassadors, by climbing round the back benches of the court, resulted in a duel in which the Russian ambassador was wounded (Nicolson, *The Evolution of Diplomatic Method*, 45). In another incident, which involved a race between the coaches of the French and Spanish ambassadors on their way to the Dutch court, when both coaches reached the walls at the same time, the gate of an alley had to be demolished so that both could pass at the same time. In retrospect the Spanish ambassador claimed

victory for passing from the right side (Hill, *A History of Diplomacy*, vol. 2, 26). Finally, even outside the so-called European society of states, one can note the performance of the *koutou* ritual, which involved the ambassador laying prostrate before the "heavenly" Chinese emperor; in many instances this Chinese protocol demand was the single, most important issue governing diplomatic relations between Western powers and China in the late eighteenth and early nineteenth century (see Robert A. Bickers, ed., *Ritual and Diplomacy: The Macartney Mission to China 1792–1794* [London: British Association for Chinese Studies, 1993]).

25. Der Derian, *Antidiplomacy*, 173–202.

26. Clifford Geertz, *Negara: The Theatre State in Nineteenth Century Bali* (Princeton, N.J.: Princeton University Press, 1980), 136.

27. Francis H. Hinsley, *Sovereignty* (Cambridge: Cambridge University Press, 1986), 3.

28. Quoted in Peter Goodrich, *Languages of Law: From Logics of Memory to Nomadic Masks* (London: Weidenfeld & Nicolson, 1990), 170.

29. See Otto Gierke, *Political Theories of the Middle Ages* (Cambridge: Cambridge University Press, 1987).

30. Karl Löwith, *Meaning in History: The Theological Presuppositions of the Philosophy of History* (Chicago: University of Chicago Press, 1949); Carl Schmitt, *Political Theology: Four Chapters on the Concept of Sovereignty* (Cambridge, Mass.: MIT Press, 1985).

31. But, after all, only the word of God can be eternal as St. Augustine teaches us: "God, in his own nature, neither begins nor ceases to speak; he speaks not temporally, but eternally." *City of God*, book X, chap. 15.

32. See Michael G. Dillon and Jerry Everard, "Stat(e)ing Australia: Squid-jigging and the Masque of State," *Alternatives* 17, no. 3 (1992): 281–312.

33. See Ernst H. Kantorowicz, *The King's Two Bodies: A Study in Mediaeval Political Theology* (Princeton, N.J.: Princeton University Press, 1957).

34. James Mayall, *Nationalism and International Society* (Cambridge: Cambridge University Press, 1990), 7.

35. For good discussions on papal representation, see Mario Oliveri, *The Representatives: The Real Nature and Function of Papal Legates* (Exeter: Van Duren, 1980); and Schmutz, "The Foundations of Medieval Papal Representation."

36. Barber, *Diplomacy: The World of the Honest Spy*, 123.

37. For further on angels, see Der Derian, *On Diplomacy*, 44–45, 65–67.

38. For further on diplomatic accounts concerning tables and seating arrangements, see Cohen, *Theatre of Power*, 132–34.

39. Nicolson, *Diplomacy*, 31.

40. Der Derian, *On Diplomacy*, 1.

41. Mikhail Bakhtin, *Rabelais and His World* (Cambridge, Mass.: MIT Press, 1968), 10.

42. Der Derian, *On Diplomacy*, 200.

43. Alienation is usually seen as "synonymous with oppression or repression" and estrangement as "a road to self-discovery." See the introduction in Michael Theunissen, *The Other: Studies in the Social Ontology of Husserl, Heidegger, Sartre and Buber* (Cambridge, Mass.: MIT Press, 1984), x.

44. Holzgrefe, "The Origins of Modern International Relations Theory," 11–26.

45. See Tzvetan Todorov, *The Conquest of America: The Question of the Other* (New York: Harper & Row, 1984), 247.

46. As argued by Sartre in Theunissen, *The Other*, 201.

47. Quoted in Adam Watson, *Diplomacy: The Dialogue between States* (London: Methuen, 1982), 14.

48. For the international legal discourse of self-determination, see Michael Akehurst, *A Modern Introduction to International Law* (London: Allen & Unwin, 1987), 290–302; and Ian Brownlie, *Principles of Public International Law* (Oxford: Clarendon, 1990), 595–98.

49. Der Derian, *On Diplomacy*, chap. 4.

50. *Pacific Islands Monthly*, March 1991.

51. Gwenda Cornell, *Pacific Odyssey* (London: Adlard Coles, 1985), 86.

52. Jacques Derrida, "Declarations of Independence," *New Political Science* 15 (1986): 7–15, 10; and for an interesting comparison with Hannah Arendt, see Bonnie Honig, "Declarations of Independence: Arendt and Derrida on the Problem of Founding a Republic," *American Political Science Review* 15, no. 1 (March 1991): 97–113.

53. See Marco Polo, *The Travels*; and "Kublai Khan: The Colossal Regal Body," in S. M. Islam, "Construction of the Others"(Ph.D. diss., University of Essex, 1982), 280–298.

54. Peter J. Boyce, *Foreign Affairs for New States: Some Questions of Credentials* (New York: St Martin's, 1977), 249.

55. Zygmunt Bauman, *Modernity and the Holocaust* (Cambridge: Polity, 1989), 162–63.

56. Lacan, *The Four Fundamental Concepts of Psycho-Analysis*, 220.

57. Frey and Frey, "Fatal Diplomacy, 1541," 10–15.

58. Cornelius Castoriadis, *The Imaginary Institution of Society* (Cambridge: Polity, 1987), 102.

59. Ibid., 105.

60. Ottaviano Maggi, *De Legato: Libri Duo* (1566), as quoted in Mattingly, *Renaissance Diplomacy*, 186.

61. Quoted in Alberico Gentili, *De Legationibus* (New York: Oxford University Press, 1924), book III, chap. 1.

62. Donald E. Queller, *The Office of Ambassador in the Middle Ages* (Princeton, N.J.: Princeton University Press, 1967), 145.

63. *Relazioni di Ambasciatori Veneti,* as summarized in Queller, *The Office of Ambassador,* 146.

64. Smith Simpson, *Education in Diplomacy: An Introduction* (Washington, D.C.: Institute for the Study of Diplomacy, Georgetown University, 1987), 26.

65. Angelos Vlahos, *Once Upon a Time a Diplomat,* vol. 1 (Athens: Hestia, 1985), 16.

66. Der Derian, *On Diplomacy,* 181.

67. Todorov, *Conquest of America,* 254.

68. Foucault, *The Order of Things,* 326.

HORS D'OEUVRE: Gastronomic Diplomacy: Commensality, Communion, Communication

1. Fatma M. Cocek, *East Encounters West: France and the Ottoman Empire in the Eighteenth Century* (Oxford: Oxford University Press, 1987), 140.

2. Edwards, *True Brits: Inside the Foreign Office,* 138.

3. For additional references on the role of food and drink in the Mediterranean region, see Fernand Braudel, *The Mediterranean and the Mediterranean World in the Age of Philip II* (London: HarperCollins, 1992).

4. Sigmund Freud, *Totem and Taboo* (London: Routledge, 1960).

5. Hans-Georg Gadamer, *Truth and Method* (London: Sheed & Ward, 1989), 124.

6. Plato, *Symposium,* 174A–176E.

7. Numelin, *The Beginnings of Diplomacy,* 203.

8. Aristotle, *Politics,* book II, 1271a, 26–1271a, 37, 1272a, 12–1272a, 26.

9. Ibid., 1252b, 19.

10. For the whole discussion, see Aristotle, *Nicomachean Ethics,* book III, 10.8–11.3.

11. Xenophon, *Memorabilia,* 2:XI, 22.

12. Aristotle, *Politics,* 1251b, 7.

13. Plato, *Gorgias,* 464 C.

14. See, e.g., Demosthenes, *De Falsa Legatione,* 414.

15. Ibid., 350.

16. Demosthenes, *Philippic II,* 30.

17. Homer, *The Iliad,* book XXIV, 552–642.

18. Quoted in Demosthenes, *De Falsa Legatione,* 400.

19. As discussed in Aeschines, *De Falsa Legatione,* 23.

20. Marcel Detienne and Jean-Pierre Vernant, *The Cuisine of Sacrifice among the Greeks* (Chicago: University of Chicago Press, 1989), 24.

21. Plato, *The Republic,* 379 E.

22. See, e.g., Thucydides, *History of the Pelopponesian War,* 1:35, 1:87, 4:16, 5:21, 5:30, 5:39, 5:9, 5:76, 6:7. See also Frank Adcock and D. J. Mosley, *Diplomacy in Ancient Greece* (London: Thames and Hudson, 1975), 200–201.

23. See further Frederick W. Dillistone, *Christianity and Symbolism* (London: SCM Press, 1955), 263.

24. See, for example, Anderson, *The Rise of Modern Diplomacy, 1450–1919.*

25. Bull, *The Anarchical Society: A Study of Order in World Politics,* 33–38.

26. Todorov, *The Conquest of America,* 154–57.

27. Peter Mason, *Deconstructing America: Representations of the Other* (London: Routledge, 1990), 53.

28. See Thomas Naff, "The Ottoman Empire and the European States," in Hedley Bull and Adam Watson, eds., *The Expansion of International Society* (Oxford: Clarendon Press, 1984), and Jacob C. Hurewitz, "Ottoman Diplomacy and the European State System," *Middle East Journal* 15 (1961): 141–52.

29. Quoted in Cocek, *East Encounters West,* 41; see 37–41 for a discussion on dining attitudes.

30. For the classic work in this area, see Norbert Elias, *The Civilizing Process: History of Manners* (Oxford: Blackwell, 1982).

31. Edwards, *True Brits,* 138.

32. Martin F. Herz, ed., *Diplomacy: The Role of the Wife* (Washington, D.C.: Institute for the Study of Diplomacy, Georgetown University, 1981), 68–69.

33. Ibid.

34. Robert J. Moore, *Third World Diplomats in Dialogue with the First World* (London: Macmillan, 1985), 38.

35. Eric Clark, *Corps Diplomatique* (London: Allen Lane, 1973), 89.

36. Cohen, *Theatre of Power,* 163.

37. Hope Cooke, *Time Change: An Autobiography* (New York: Simon and Schuster, 1980), 158.

38. Ibid.

39. George Lanitis, "Diplomatic Gastronomy," *Cyprus Diplomatist* 1 (January-February 1989): 94–95; emphasis added.

40. Gandhian fasting has been addressed in Bhikhu Parekh, *Gandhi's Political Philosophy: A Critical Examination* (London: Macmillan, 1989).

POSTMORTEM: The Revelation of Hermes

1. For a recent catechism on postmodernism, see Fred Halliday, *Rethinking International Relations* (London: Macmillan, 1994), 37–46.

2. Ibid., 38.

3. See Bauman, *Modernity and the Holocaust*.

4. For an exemplification of this point, see David Campbell, *Politics without Principle: Sovereignty, Ethics, and the Narratives of the Gulf War* (Boulder: Lynne Rienner, 1993), chap. 5 and 6.

5. See Walker, *Inside/Outside*; Der Derian, *Antidiplomacy*; Der Derian, ed., *International Theory: Critical Investigations*; George, *Discourses of Global Politics*.

6. On chronopolitics, see Paul Virilio, *Speed and Politics: An Essay on Dromology* (New York: Semiotext[e], 1986), and for its IR application, Der Derian, "The (S)pace of International Relations," in *Antidiplomacy*.

7. Plato, *Gorgias*, 521 D.

8. Ibid., 474 A.

9. For a detailed psychoanalytical study of this Hermetic function, see Karoly Kerenyi, *Hermes: Guide of Souls* (New York: Spring Books, 1976).

10. Nicolson, *Diplomacy*, 6–7.

11. *The Homeric Hymn to Hermes*, 286.

12. For the story of how Hermes deceived both Zeus and Apollo, see ibid.

13. *The Homeric Hymn to Hermes*, 115–37.

14. See Garth Fowden, *The Egyptian Hermes: A Historical Approach to the Late Pagan Mind* (Princeton, N.J.: Princeton University Press, 1986).

15. Caputo, *Radical Hermeneutics*, 153.

16. Derrida, *Dissemination*, 86.

17. I refer here to the task of interpretation and not to a specific hermeneutical approach (for example, following Edmund Husserl, Martin Heidegger, Hans-Georg Gadamer, or the Frankfurt School in general). For a good review of the different hermeneutical approaches, see Caputo, *Radical Hermeneutics*.

18. Heraclitus, *Fragments*, xi.

19. An example of such messages is the *ixis aphixeis ou en to polemo thnixeis* (you go you return not die in war), changing meaning according to where the comma is put. Another classical example is Pyrrhus who suffered by giving a specific interpretation to the prophecy. For these and many other examples, see Angelos Vlahos, *Pythias Paraleremata* (Athens: Hestia, 1983).

20. Many examples of these in Thucydides, *History of the Pelopponesian War*. See also Demosthenes's suggestion of the Philipization of Pythia (noting the Macedonian influence over the Delphic oracle) in Vlahos, *Pythias Paraleremata*.

Index

Costas M. Constantinou is lecturer in international politics at the University of Hull. His essays have been published in *Alternatives, Millennium,* and the *Cyprus Review.*